After the Breakup

Women Sort through the Rubble and Rebuild Lives of New Possibilities

ANGELA WATROUS
CAROLE HONEYCHURCH, M.A.

MJF BOOKS
NEW YORK

Published by MJF Books
Fine Communications
Two Lincoln Square
60 West 66th Street
New York, NY 10023

After the Breakup
LC Control Number 2001119318
ISBN 1-56731-502-X

Manufactured in the United States of America on acid-free paper ∞

MJF Books and the MJF colophon are trademarks of Fine Creative Media, Inc.

BG   10 9   8   7   6   5   4   3   2   1

Dwell in possibility.

—Emily Dickinson

*All you can do is arm yourself
with other women's stories.*

—Ophira Edut

*As long as we allow breakup
terror to shape all our tomorrows,
our own ability to storytell whatever
future we want will be sadly limited.*

—Marny Hall

Contents

Part II Rebuilding

Part III Settling In

Acknowledgments

We'd like to thank all the folks at New Harbinger Publications, especially Matthew McKay and Kristin Beck for providing us with the opportunity to make this project a reality, and Farrin Jacobs for her skillful editing. Thank you Amy Shoup, Lauren Dockett, Michele Waters, Kirk Johnson, Gretchen Gold, Catharine Sutker, and Heather Garnos—we appreciate the contributions each of you made to this book. Special thanks to Eileen Clegg for sharing her wisdom and for supporting us throughout the process.

Our deep gratitude and admiration go out to all of the women whose stories are the heart of this book. We were touched by your generosity and openness both with us and each other.

Thanks to my firebrand co-author for her sensitivity, chutzpah, and perseverance. Your talent and skill lofted us over many of our highest hurdles while your joke-crackin' joie de vivre made the process fun.

Thanks also to my other wonderful friends whose support and enthusiasm buoyed me up throughout the book-writing process. Erika Papakipos, thank you for sixteen years of inspiration. Thank you, Kristin Beck, for your radiant example and warm support. Steve Erickson, thank you for all you've taught me and for your steadfast love and friendship.

Much love and many thanks to my mom, Joyce Honeychurch, whose example and encouragement helped make this book what it is.

Finally, thank you, Jon Rubin, for your constant, loving support and for the faith and understanding to help push me through the rough times. This book is for you.

—C.H.

My utmost thanks go to my spirited and brainy co-author for teaching me that no matter how much work there is to be done, there's always time for laughter and dancing. Throughout this project I've been astounded by your poise, uplifted by your persistence, and ever grateful for your unwavering support.

I'd like to express my love and gratitude to my dad, Harry Watrous, for his constant encouragement, wry humor, and invaluable friendship. I'm immensely grateful to my grandma, Bessie Watrous, and to all the members of my family, for a lifetime of love and care.

Thank you Tanya Gamby, Erin Merk, Kitty Nguyen, Melissa Nunes, and Sherri Souza: Each of you have touched my life with your compassion, humor, intelligence, and steadfast support. Finally, thanks to Rachel Michaelsen for her patient guidance, and for teaching me to revel in the process of life.

—A.W.

Introduction

If you're holding this book in your hands right now, chances are you're in pain from a recent breakup. Things may seem to be spinning out of control. The life you knew a short while back may no longer be the life you're living. Don't worry. It's going to be okay. We know, because we've been through similar pain and have found that our breakups, as hard as they were at first, turned out to be the starting point for a rejuvenation and rebuilding of our selves.

Where We're Coming From

The idea for this book came about when both of us, within six months of each other, ended significant relationships. Together, we worked through our breakups, from the initial shock to the rebuilding of our respective lives. As we sorted through our emotions, which ran the gamut—failure, disbelief, sadness, relief, exhilaration, depression, anger, frustration, anticipation, resentment, acceptance— we found that these emotions didn't follow the linear order we expected. What we realized about breakups is that one day you feel nonchalant, and the next you're seething with anger or trapped in a pit of depression.

Even as we began to see all of the freedom and opportunity our breakups had granted us, we found that we would "slip," experiencing emotions we'd thought were behind us. At first, it made us angry at ourselves: We were independent, strong, intelligent women. Why couldn't we just get over this already? Why were we retreading the same old emotional ground? Did this mean we were weak? We finally realized that, as long as we were processing our thoughts and feelings—by thinking, reading, writing, and talking them out—there was no "right" way to feel. Our feelings, as unwelcome as they sometimes were, were a part of ourselves that we needed to accept and deal with.

Rather than continuing to be angry or frustrated at ourselves or trying to stick to an imaginary deadline as to when we were expected to "move on," we began to respect the process itself. We discovered that we could allow our emotions to guide us in sorting through emotional baggage. Talking to each other—especially about how confused we were by our mixed-up flow of emotions—provided us both with the realization that there was no one way to get over a breakup: each person needs to do it in her own way. Sharing our breakup experiences allowed us to learn from each other while providing us with necessary reassurance and comfort.

Because we realize that not everyone happens to have friends going through parallel breakups, because we were curious about the postbreakup strategies of other women, because we wanted to see what kind of formal research was being done on nonmarital breakups, and because we knew we still had issues of our own to work out (it's a long and dimly lit road for all of us), we wanted to write a breakup book that empathizes with, encourages, and empowers women to emerge from breakups with the best selves they've ever known.

An Opportunity to Rebuild

In this day and age, it's not uncommon for couples to have significant relationships without getting legally married. Some women live with their partners intending to get married someday. Others say they no longer believe in the institution of marriage. And for lesbian couples, legal marriage is not widely available. Yet many of the women we talked to lived with their partners, sharing the same responsibilities and level of commitment as most married couples. Some owned houses with their partners, and others had children with them.

Despite all of the evidence pointing toward the difficulties of nonmarital breakups, we noticed a difference in the support for women who were breaking up versus women who were getting legally divorced. Many of the women we spoke to mentioned having their breakups downplayed or ignored by their family, co-workers, and acquaintances. Several of the women were all too familiar with the phrase "at least you weren't married," implying that their experiences weren't as significant, life altering, or painful.

We knew this wasn't the case. As part of the ever-growing number of women in relationships that aren't legally binding, we realized how emotionally, financially, and socially difficult it is to work through a breakup.

We headed to the bookstore to see what was out there for women like us but found relatively few books on the subject of nonmarital breakups. We weren't interested in reading divorce books that neglected our experience (which in many ways was similar to divorce, though not exactly the same) by addressing only those who are legally married. The majority of the books that did address nonmarital breakups were about deciding whether to break up or getting through that first painful stage, neglecting the equally important middle and later stages of breakups. Some addressed postrelationship issues humorously, and while we appreciate and have taken great advantage of the healing power of laughter, we also value the importance of serious introspection and allowing ourselves room to grieve. Many relationship books had a chapter or section about breakups, but we knew there was more to say on the subject.

The handful of remaining books on the shelves treated breakups solely as a crisis to get through. While we agree that it's difficult to go through the breakup of a significant relationship, we also see the experience as a chance to re-vision your life and an opportunity to rebuild. We were also dismayed that few of the books we found included women who are lesbian or bisexual. We wanted this book to be a resource for *all* women going through a breakup, and we selected our interviewees accordingly. In short, we set out to write this book because we want you to know that you're not alone, that you don't have to simply laugh this off, and that you will come through this. Not only will you survive, but in the end, you can and will be a stronger, more independent, more self-aware you.

What's in This Book and Why

Because we see other women as a source for knowledge and information, we wanted to write a book that tapped into the wisdom everyday women possess. Women typically talk to each other extensively about their relationships—current, ending, and past—and view their female friends as a primary resource for exchanging support, ideas, and comfort. There's power in these exchanges. You can go to your friends to see how they've handled similar situations, get a reality check, and be reassured that your feelings are normal and valid. Whether you need to laugh, vent, cry, be comforted, slam your ex, or ask for advice on how to handle a particular problem, talking with your friends is probably one of the most useful resources you'll have.

However, the details of every breakup are different. You may have friends who've never had similar experiences or who haven't been through a breakup recently enough to remember all of the details. And some women find themselves less connected to their friends due to the extensive time and energy they've been putting into their romantic relationships. Because of this, we've tried to expand this resource of women's wisdom for you, interviewing dozens of women about their breakup experiences. These women are not the chosen few who've made it through. They are everyday women, and the progress each of them has made can be achieved by anyone. Think of them as an extended group of friends who've been through situations similar to yours and who want to share their experiences with you to help you make the most of this dynamic life transition.

We also see the value of more formal research. Psychologists have begun to explore nonmarital breakups, and in this book we'll combine their findings and theories and the experience-based theories of women who've been through breakups to provide you with the most comprehensive resource possible.

From Ground Zero to Settling In

We envision breakups as a sort of demolition and reconstruction process. The past relationship is like a condemned building: for some reason it's no longer habitable, and someone has called for the wrecking ball. Whether you planned it or not, you suddenly find yourself in the midst of the resulting rubble. In this book, we hope to provide you with the strength, wisdom, inspiration, and tools needed to clear out the debris and reconstruct a life of your own design.

In part I, "Ground Zero," we'll discuss how a breakup can be similar to a wrecking ball that comes through and levels your life. Even the women who anticipated or instigated the breakup found themselves sitting amidst the rubble, wondering what to do next. Your identity as part of a couple, or as part of that particular couple, is gone. You may have to move (if you lived with your partner), reconnect with friends (if you've drifted away from them), make use of creative financing (if you combined your finances with your partner's), and reassess multiple other aspects of your self-concept and your daily life.

It isn't easy to sort through the rubble, trying to find what is salvageable. You may find that some of the most precious aspects of your life have been destroyed or no longer bring you joy or satisfaction. It's painful to consider what is left and what is no longer, and it may be tempting to try to rebuild right over the debris, ignoring its existence. However, in order to reconstruct a structurally sound life, you must clear away the rubble and create a solid foundation. It takes time, it takes work—but it's your life, and you deserve the stability and comfort that rebuilding from the ground up will bring you.

In part II, "Rebuilding," we'll discuss how women redesigned and reconstructed their new life. This process is one of the most exciting and rewarding parts of ending a relationship. (Don't believe anyone who insinuates that it's *all* hard and painful.) What have you always wanted to do? Where have you always wanted to live? The demolition brought on by a breakup also creates open space you can use to revise your identity, do things just for yourself, and make self-gratifying, you-based decisions. Think of yourself as a talented architect with a unique vision—you're going to design your life, to your specifications.

You won't have to wait until your design is complete to begin rebuilding. After all, this is a metaphorical building we're talking about. Life isn't a cut-and-dried process. Most of the women we talked to mentioned finding postbreakup debris throughout the process, so try not to be too surprised or hard on yourself if you find yourself sitting in the middle of your new life, crying over a memory from the past or throwing darts (mentally or literally) at a picture of your ex. It's natural to expect that you'll still have some kind of feelings for anyone who's been a significant part of your life long after your relationship has changed. As time goes on, you'll encounter less and less of the rubble, but it's always possible to find bits and pieces, no matter how much time has passed.

In part III, "Settling In," you'll see how becoming comfortable in your new life often brings some level of closure to your past relationship. The women we interviewed talk about how and if they've experienced closure, how to get there, and how to know when you've arrived. We'll help you come to terms with the fact that a breakup, though it rarely seems so at first, is always a positive transition that eventually facilitates positive change.

As you settle in, you may find that you have a renewed energy and *joie de vivre*. The energy you've put into maintaining and then getting over your past relationship will finally be available for yourself—to use however you want. Whether you choose to explore a new city, work on a new project, enjoy a new relationship, or all of these things and more, you'll learn how to transform your breakup from a crisis that causes your life to grind to a halt into the opportunity of your lifetime.

By the end of the process, we hope that you will feel at home in your rebuilt life, and can use that place of belonging and comfort to soar to heights previously unimaginable.

Part I

Ground Zero

Standing amidst
the Rubble

It's so scary. It's like taking this huge leap, and it feels like a long time before you hit the ground.

—Jeanette

I couldn't figure out what was wrong with me. Just when I would think, "This is it. I'm finally over this," I would find myself in the pit of depression or seething with rage.

—Lily

Everything was completely up in the air, as if dynamite had gone off and destroyed everything.

—Renee

Even if you saw it coming or made it happen, you may find yourself unprepared for the initial impact of your breakup. Suddenly, you're no longer half of a couple. You may not know who to turn to. Everything around you—your home, your favorite music, your loved ones—may seem connected to your ex.

We liken this early stage of the breakup to finding yourself at "ground zero." It can feel as if a wrecking ball has slammed into your life. Things that you took for granted yesterday may no longer apply to your life today. Everything is changing at a rapid and unstoppable pace. Much of the life you've constructed has been reduced to rubble. While *you* are still intact, many of your dreams and plans for the future, as well as your day-to-day existence, may suddenly be unrecognizable bits and pieces.

Ground zero is also a place for beginnings. While your relationship has ended, you are embarking on a new journey. This can be terrifying at first. Maybe you liked the way your life was before, and you feel resistant to all the changes that a breakup can bring. Or maybe you felt comfortable with the way things were, even if you were unhappy. The known generally feels safer than the unknown, regardless of the situation. Jeanette had thought she would be with Chris forever and that she had a good idea of what the future held for her. Though their interests and career goals differed widely, and she often felt she was settling with some of his shortcomings, she had made up her mind that Chris was "the one." When they had grown apart to the degree that they were basically leading separate lives, she decided to end the seven-year relationship. Though the breakup was two years ago, twenty-four-year-old Jeanette still remembers the feeling of insecurity she felt, almost as if she was stepping into an unknowable abyss:

It's so scary. It's like taking this huge leap, and it feels like a long time before you hit the ground.

Because it's difficult to have any kind of perspective at the beginning of your breakup, and because hindsight is twenty-twenty, we asked some of the women we interviewed to share what they now know that they wish they'd known at the very beginning of their breakups. Jeanette talked about how uncertain she'd felt that she would ever get over the pain of her breakup:

I distinctly remember my dad telling me, "I know it doesn't seem like it now, but there will be a time when this lessens and lessens, and it just happens, and you'll be okay." And I just thought, "You don't understand what I'm going through." I couldn't even imagine how things could get better. Then, six months later, my friend broke up with her partner, and I told her what my dad had said, and I said, "I know it sounds like a bunch of shit, but it's really true."

I also wish I'd realized at the beginning that it was okay that I didn't believe what he said, because I needed to learn it for myself. I needed to have that experience and prove it to myself. At the time, everything in my life seemed connected to Chris. But as I eventually had new experiences in my life, there became all of these things that were not at all connected to him—it just took time and doing other things to put space between us.

Just before her breakup, Miranda found out that her mother had cancer. She'd counted on her partner of four years to help her get through the crisis. When the relationship fell apart, she wondered how on earth she was going to get through both experiences at the same time. She pulled through with strength and creativity, and now, four years later, she can look back at those hard times and see how far she's come. She speculated about how much easier it would be if you could actually see into the future when your breakup hits: "I wish I'd known that it would be okay, eventually. That I'd get through it and be better for it."

Many women find the assurance that they will survive hackneyed or irritating at the beginning of their breakups. It can seem as if no one can truly understand your pain becuase your experience is unique—and in some ways, of course, it is. But as we spoke to more and more women, we found that all of the women who'd gained the perspective that time brings (as well as many of those still at ground zero) felt that their breakups provided them with a bounty of new possibilities in their lives.

Of course, we don't want to diminish the fact that being at ground zero (and even the rebuilding stage after a breakup) can be an excruciating and wrenching experience. Though most of the women we've talked to look back at their breakups as positive experiences, none of them said it was easy, especially in the beginning. When thirty-year-old Sarah had to end her relationship four years ago, she found herself questioning if it was normal to be having such a hard time: "I wish I'd known that I would go through depression and a lot of pain; I always thought there was something wrong with me because it was so hard."

Sarah's experience is common. Many women are taken by surprise, even if they've experienced other significant breakups, by how hard and painful a breakup can be. Because you'll likely have to continue functioning on a day-to-day basis—going to work or school, taking care of the kids, paying your bills—you may have to put up an emotional front in some parts of your life. This reality can conflict with the tremendous feelings of loss and grief you may be experiencing.

During this time, try not to be too hard on yourself. Everyone responds differently to a breakup, and there is no right or wrong way to react. It may not seem like it now, but you will get through this and come out the other side. And, eventually, you may begin to see that other side as brighter.

Sorting through the Rubble

It's easy to obsess on why a relationship doesn't work out. You may be asking yourself questions like "What did I do wrong? What could I have done differently? What would have happened if I'd tried a different tactic?" In *The Lesbian Couple's Guide*, author Judith McDaniel challenges this thinking, and her words can be applied to women of all sexual orientations:

"Especially as women, we tend to think that if a relationship isn't working it's because we didn't put enough effort into it initially, or because we haven't learned enough yet. Any of these things could be true, but generally, I've found, they're not. Relationships don't work because we're basically incompatible with the woman to whom we're (inexplicably) drawn. They don't work because we've grown in different directions from the woman we started down the road with. They don't work because we take them too seriously, rarely the opposite." (235)

Especially while you're in the initial stages of your breakup, you may be overwhelmed with "whys" and "what-ifs" and feel as though the ending of your relationship has left you stranded in uncharted territory. It may seem like you're the only one who has experienced something so painful and no one could possibly understand your devastation. You may feel pressure—from yourself or others—to move on and get over it.

But before you can begin to move on, you must sort through the rubble left from your breakup, choosing what to salvage and what to leave behind. By identifying what went wrong, what your part in it was, and how you'd like things to be different in the future, you can better ensure that you won't find yourself in the same situation in future relationships. You might be tempted to try to rebuild right over the debris, because assessing your past and reconciling it with your present and future isn't easy. But, as the women we spoke to can attest, skipping over this process can leave you with a shaky foundation.

One reason why breaking up is so difficult to negotiate—with ourselves, our exes, and our communities—is that there are no concrete rules for how a breakup is supposed to progress. In *Uncoupling*, Diane Vaughan blames this difficulty on the lack of exposure to breakups in our society. While there are a lot of rituals and rites for how to be a couple, very few exist for how to break up. We may have no idea how our lives will shape up after our breakups, having very few examples to follow.

We've all heard countless stories of burgeoning romances, but there aren't a lot of vivid depictions of what it's like to go through the entire process of a breakup. A breakup doesn't make as good a story as the beginning of a relationship does, because relationships come about from a climax in events—meeting someone, going out with him or her, and making a mutual decision to be together. While the act of breaking up also has an initial climactic element, the resolution of a breakup is more like a fading over time, an internal process that may not have a finite ending. We may always have some feeling about our ex-lovers or the breakup experience, no matter how many years or other relationships have passed.

This lack of conventional wisdom can leave us with less of a sense of how a breakup actually works, making it especially important to learn about the experiences of other women. Of course, there isn't one right way to go through a breakup, so it's also important to try to be accepting of yourself as you go through the process. Talking to those you trust about your feelings all through your postbreakup experience can help you get some perspective on this rapidly changing and confusing time.

Being at ground zero can feel pretty bleak. While we don't want to diminish the significance of this phase, we want to continually emphasize what we learned from the women we interviewed: rejuvenation will come—you just need to hold on, take care of yourself, and allow yourself time for introspection. Remember that while you're in the midst of an ending, you're also at the onset of a beginning. Diane Vaughan reminds us that all breakups involve a shift in our self-perception and our world view that offers the potential for redefining ourselves."

Am I the Only One Who Feels Like This?

When we began searching for women to interview, one of the things we discovered right away was that everyone seemed to feel alone in her postbreakup process. Many women said they'd be happy to help, except that they felt their breakups were kind of unusual. It wasn't uncommon for individual women to feel that their breakups were the most humiliating, the most bizarre, the most wrenching, and that because of that their experiences wouldn't be as helpful to other women.

During the interview groups, however, it quickly became clear that experiencing different circumstances didn't prevent the women from relating to each other's stories. While the intensity of emotions sometimes varied—due to the circumstances, the length of time that had passed, and individual personalities—there were many common emotions and shared reactions. Even the women who'd thought their circumstances were unusual found that they had things to share that resonated with the group.

One of the common threads in the groups was the experience of strong feelings of grief. Many of the women said the grief they experienced following their breakups felt just like they were coping with the death of a partner or other loved one. A few even felt that a death would have been easier to accept. Twenty-eight-year-old Lily discovered that her partner had another girlfriend on the side and had returned to his former circle of friends when she found a letter he'd written to the woman. She talked about the grief she experienced after discovering that her ex was a "psychopathic liar."

It was even worse than if he'd died. This way, I had to deal with losing him, our relationship, and that part of my life, but on top of that I had the humiliation of his lies and betrayal. If he'd died, I would have been devastated, but at least I wouldn't have felt like such a fucking idiot.

Our review of professional literature supported what we heard from the women in the interview groups—that breakups generally result in a time of intense grieving. Just like any substantial loss, a breakup creates the need to mourn, acknowledge loss, and let go.

The grieving process can involve a gamut of emotions, so we asked the women we interviewed about the emotions they experienced most intensely after their breakups. Even though thirty-nine-year-old Barbara initiated her breakup in order to have more space and freedom to meet her own needs and tend to her career as an artist, she still suffered from an almost visceral experience of shock:

*It was just terrible. It literally felt like an umbilical cord had been cut. I
felt like I was bleeding. Even though I knew I had to do it, I just felt
like I was hemorrhaging. There was some place inside me where I knew
it was the right thing to do. But at that moment I could only think,
"What have I done?"*

One morning as forty-three-year-old Renee was leaving for
work she kissed Bree, her partner of fifteen years, good-bye as usual.
When she got no response, she told Bree, "Sometimes it just doesn't
feel like you love me anymore." Bree simply replied, "Go to work."
Later that day, Bree admitted that she was leaving the relationship to
be with another woman. Renee told us:

*I'll never forget that feeling when she said, "That's right. I'm leaving
you." I was looking at a glass of water on the coffee table and I
thought, I should be able to make that water boil, I'm feeling such
incredible emotion. Just the most amazing shock.*

While shock is especially common directly after a breakup, it
can sneak up at other times too: when you wake up in bed and realize for the hundredth time that your partner is no longer next to you,
when someone who is unaware of the breakup asks how your partner is doing, or when you encounter the million daily reminders that
your breakup is in fact a reality.

A discussion of grief wouldn't be complete without talking
about the deep feelings of sadness that come with any serious loss.
But perhaps "sadness" really isn't the right word. While sadness is a
common component to psychologists' definitions of grief, none of the
women we interviewed used the word "sad" to describe their postbreakup emotions. Instead, they talked about experiencing bouts of
depression and often overwhelming feelings of gut-wrenching sorrow. Sadness doesn't seem to fully convey the strength of the feelings
women experience after the end of a significant relationship. While
professionals would make a distinction between sadness (or
depressed mood) and clinical depression, the women we spoke to
used stronger language, trying to best convey the intensity of their
emotions.

Psychologists also talk about a sense of relief that grieving people are sometimes surprised to encounter, and several women in our
groups did talk about the relief brought on by their breakups.

Hannah, who had been thinking of leaving her live-in boyfriend for about a year before the situation became untenable, was overwhelmed with both a great sadness and a strange sense of relief when she finally broke the news two years ago:

God, it was so strange. He just cracked in front of my eyes, sort of sagging and saying, "I don't think you like me anymore." Then I just had to tell him that I wanted to leave, and afterward we sat on the couch and talked about it for a long time. The funny thing about it was, even though I felt so awful that it was finally ending, it also felt so good to finally be doing something about it. But it was almost otherworldly—I almost felt as if my head was floating above my body as we talked. I felt that relieved.

If you were arguing a lot with your partner, if you felt stifled in your relationship, or if you sensed that something was coming for quite some time, relief may be one of your primary reactions.

You may also find that you experience guilt after your breakup. Clare's partner guilt-tripped her into believing that he was the injured party, even though he was the one breaking up. He blamed her for their increasingly frequent arguments and refused to take responsibility for any of the problems they were having. It wasn't until later that Clare found out her ex had been interested in someone else, whom he started dating several weeks after their breakup:

For that week when we were breaking up, I was taking care of him. I felt really bad about myself. You know, I blamed myself for the whole thing. Now I think, "What the fuck was I doing?!"

Lily initially felt wracked with guilt, even though she'd discovered that her partner had cheated on her for the last six months of their four-year relationship. He claimed that he'd only lied to her because he'd been devastated when she'd told him the year before that she thought she was bisexual. Even though three years have passed, Lily still feels conflicted about her feelings of guilt:

I know I hurt him. His mom had come out to him the year before we started dating, and he'd never fully accepted that she was a lesbian. So I think it just freaked him out when I told him that I undeniably had this all-consuming crush on a woman. I can understand that he felt betrayed and threatened—we both knew that it was a threat to our relationship. But over the past three years I've realized that there was a difference between how I hurt him and how he hurt me. I hurt him—without wanting to—by being honest, but he hurt me on purpose by lying to me.

Especially right after a breakup, it's not uncommon to feel guilty for your part in the failure of the relationship. Your feelings may change over time as you gain perspective or learn more information, or you may eventually have to forgive yourself for things you wish you'd done differently.

Anger is another common component of the grief process. After Lee's partner called her at work to break up with her, he refused to have any communication with her to explain his reasons. Even though they'd been together for only four months, they had been good friends before the romance, and Lee was outraged at the lack of explanation:

After we broke up, I was having these moments of getting really excited about my future. Maybe I brought this relationship into my life to distract myself. And then the other night I was just getting pissed. It was shocking to me how one minute I could be thinking, "I'm so glad I'm finally working through these issues, this is so cool," and then the next minute be so angry.

The changeability and intensity of the emotions triggered by a breakup can feel unsettling. While it's important to acknowledge your feelings of anger, it's generally best not to act on them. So how do you deal with all that pent-up rage? Well, the women we spoke to had a variety of suggestions, including kickboxing classes, writing angry letters to your ex that you don't send, and the tried-and-true throwing darts at or otherwise mutilating your ex's picture. You can probably also expect many angry ranting sessions with your friends, and maybe some furious pillow-punching. But, perhaps the best advice the women in our groups could offer about anger was to remember that, like the other negative emotions that flood you after a breakup, it *will* fade.

Because women have traditionally been socialized not to express anger, we may be more likely to take it out on ourselves or repress it. When Anne's partner, Jill, started spending more and more time with Jill's devoutly Mormon family, Anne began to suspect that Jill was considering converting. As Anne did not want any part of organized religion, she expressed her concerns. After months of Jill insisting that nothing was changing, Anne ran across photos of Jill's recent and covert baptism. Anne talked about how her anger about the breakup has been directed largely toward herself: "I get mad at myself: 'Goddamn, why didn't you see it? Why weren't you stronger, why didn't you get out of it sooner?'" It's easy to berate ourselves with "whys," but turning anger in on ourselves can only make us feel worse, resulting in feelings of low self-esteem, worthlessness, or depression. It may help to acknowledge anger and express it in constructive ways, treating yourself with understanding and compassion while you wait out this phase.

You may also experience intense longing for the comfort and security that you once had from your relationship. Hannah, who came down with the stomach flu soon after her breakup, really missed the safety and security she felt with her former partner:

There I was, sick as a dog, and what I really wanted was for someone to put a cold cloth on my head, cook me some broth, and run out and get me some movies—things he used to do for me. I think that was the lowest point—and the point where I missed him the most.

Longing can make you feel compelled to reunite with your ex or jump into another relationship. It can be scary at first to face the world without a partner. But if you allow yourself to feel your fear and your longing and really sit with those emotions, you will eventually come to terms with your feelings. The strength and independence that you can find through doing this is much more stable and satisfying than being with someone because you feel you can't be alone.

Especially right after a breakup, the grief can seem unbearable, and it can be hard to believe that it won't last forever. Many women said they'd had difficulty keeping up with the daily tasks of life, such as going to work, walking the dog, paying the bills—even just getting out of bed. It can all feel pretty overwhelming while you're immersed in grieving your loss. But it does get better over time. Every single woman we spoke to eventually saw some relief from her pain—even the women we interviewed who'd only been out of their relationships for a few weeks or months. And all of the women who felt they'd fully grieved their past relationships were able to move on to fulfilling new lives.

Two Steps Forward,
One Step Back

Early psychological research suggested that the stages of grief were somewhat predictable and linear, and this myth prevails in our culture and in many of our minds. But later research, as well as real women's experiences, disprove this theory. Many of the women we interviewed were surprised that their feelings were changing so rapidly and sporadically. It can be confusing to feel perfectly fine for days, and then suddenly find yourself longing for your ex or overwhelmed with guilt, though your circumstances may not have changed at all. Lily, unaware that this was a normal stage of the process, berated herself for her chaotic emotions:

I couldn't figure out what was wrong with me. Just when I would think, "This is it. I'm finally over this," I would find myself in the pit of depression or seething with rage. I was so angry at my ex, but I was also incredibly lonely and I missed the comfort of our relationship. I kept thinking I was moving backwards, and I was really down on myself because of it. This went on and on, until I finally mentioned how frustrated I was to a friend. Turned out she'd had the same experience after one of her breakups, and she'd thought she was doing something wrong, too.

Even after time passes and you begin to move on with your life, old emotions may creep up on you when you least expect it. When Sarah called up her ex to ask him which inoculations they'd had before the last trip they'd taken together, she wasn't prepared for the emotions it would dredge up in her:

I called and he'd changed his number to his new girlfriend's place. I called and I heard her voice on the machine. I had to leave a message and I could hear my voice shaking. And I was so mad at myself—both that my voice was shaking and that the new person with him would hear my voice shaking! I thought that it was ridiculous—I mean, it's been three years. Why is my voice shaking?

While it's common to wish our emotions were under our control, breakups can be a constant reminder that they're not. Grieving the loss of those who were important in our lives is a messy process. It doesn't fit any timetable or logical flow. Accepting that this is just the way it is can help keep us from blaming ourselves for not meeting our own unrealistic expectations.

A Beginning, a Middle, and an End

One of the things we discovered from our interviews was that the postbreakup experience seems to have three different phases. First there's ground zero, the time directly after the breakup when emotions are intense and immobilizing. This is followed by a period of rebuilding, when the past is worked out and the future is worked toward. Finally, there comes a point when all of the hard work pays off and we're comfortable enough to settle in to the present and freely move forward.

The women we talked to all experienced some level of shock and disorientation at ground zero. Thirty-year-old Lucy's partner of eighteen months broke up with her after reading her journal, in which she described her increasing feelings of attraction to another man. Though she'd been wavering about the relationship for some time, nothing prepared her for what the time right after her breakup would really be like:

I just remember going to movies by myself all the time and lying on my floor and crying, and constantly feeling that wrenching feeling. I couldn't believe this person I was so close to was gone. It was like having my arm ripped off. But there was a part of me that kept saying, "Go, go, go, go, go, just don't look back."

Many of the women talked of experiencing several different emotions at once, often in conflict with one another. Occasional feelings of relief didn't seem to lessen feelings of longing, anger coexisted with guilt, and time seemed to move differently than usual. Renee talked about how she experienced ground zero after her breakup five years ago:

It was so interesting to have all of those reactions at the same time. There was relief—"Yes, this is right. This is for the best." And then, "Oh, my god. All of my future has just gone out the door." Everything was completely up in the air, as if dynamite had gone off and destroyed everything.

The shock following a breakup seemed to be the most commonly shared experience among the women we interviewed, even for women who instigated the ending or knew that the relationship was flailing.

Forty-eight-year-old Denise's partner, Mary, had been acting strangely for quite some time. As Mary began spending more and more time with a male colleague, Denise became suspicious and asked if there was anything going on between them. Mary denied that they were anything but friends and acted outraged that Denise would even suggest such a thing. But as time went on, Mary became increasingly distant. One day Mary finally admitted that she was leaving Denise for a man, and that she was unwilling to even try to work things out. Although it didn't come as a complete surprise, Denise was still in shock:

It's not like I didn't know something wasn't right—but we were married. I thought we were going to spend the rest of our lives together. I thought we were just going through some changes. There was never a discussion about "This isn't working." So when she finally said, "I'm at a turning point in our relationship. I can't be in our relationship anymore," I was like, "Hello! What are you talking about? We have a four-year-old, we have three kids amongst us, we have pets, we have this house. You're insane." Suddenly my life was just flashing before my eyes.

Maria's partner, Terri, ended their fourteen-year relationship ten years ago when Maria expressed her skepticism regarding Terri's sudden belief that her father had molested her as a young girl. While Maria wanted to be supportive, she found it difficult because Terri had no actual memories of abuse, rather her therapist had suggested that Terri must have been abused due to other factors in her life. While Maria was at ground zero, she couldn't recognize any potential benefits to her breakup:

I was so devastated. I just wanted to self-destruct. The worst thing was that it was completely out of my control. I had built my sense of security in the world around being in this relationship.

Even those women who felt demolished eventually moved on as their pain lessened and new people and opportunities filled the space left by their breakups. But at ground zero it's sometimes difficult to imagine that the pain will ever go away.

One way that many women help alleviate the pain caused by the finality of a breakup is to keep the possibility of a reunion in the backs of their minds. Thirty-year-old Eden found that contemplating a reunion with her ex helped her get through the loneliness she experienced early on:

I never quite believed that we would be apart forever, and that really helped, especially in the beginning. It was so comforting to call him Friday or Saturday night, when we were both alone, and have a sort of drunken, mushy conversation.

Many of the women we talked to used this strategy to lessen the pain during the transition but found that once they had rebuilt their lives, they were no longer interested in a romantic relationship with their ex. A few women we spoke to did eventually get back together with their partners, though they all expressed that the time apart was invaluable.

During the beginning of a breakup, feelings of social isolation are also common. Jeanette talked about the predicament she found herself in after her breakup:

I'd been so immersed in this failing relationship that I'd been neglecting my friendships for months. After the breakup, I really needed my friends' support, but I was ashamed to call them. I didn't want to be one of those people who only call because they need something. But I had to bite the bullet and call, and when I did, none of them guilt-tripped me. They were all incredibly supportive and loving. It really showed me how important they were in my life.

Support from friends and loved ones was vital for the women we interviewed in getting through ground zero. It can be immeasurably helpful to reach out to others and ask for help in getting through this process.

As the initial shock and chaos of ground zero dies down, we eventually begin to piece our lives back together and make decisions about what we'd like to change. The rebuilding stage can feel daunting, but it also offers a wide array of possibilities that previously seemed unavailable or low priority in the context of our relationships. During this time, we have the opportunity to make changes in ourselves, our community, and our material world. We can revise our goals and dreams for the future, invest time in new interests or activities, revamp our social lives.

When twenty-seven-year-old Lee's relationship ended two weeks ago, it triggered her desire to address issues that had been plaguing her for years:

With this last relationship, a lot of my own stuff came up, and I just thought, you know what, this stuff has been coming up my whole life in every relationship I've had, and I want to deal with it right now. Although my pride has been hurt, I also feel really excited. This breakup has given me a great opportunity to work on these things that I've needed to work on, wanted to work on, but never quite had the push to get myself through. This breakup gave me the push.

Forty-four-year-old Rachel's partner, Linda, had been debilitated with epileptic seizures for several months toward the end of their fifteen-year relationship. Rachel focused her energies on taking care of Linda, at the expense of her own free time and social connections. As soon as Linda got back on her feet two months ago, she informed Rachel that she was leaving her to be with a woman Linda had previously insisted was just a friend. Though it'd only been one month since her unexpected breakup, Rachel already had a sense of the possibilities to come:

There are positive things. Not having to live with someone who is dependent on me all the time, someone who weighs me down. I sort of feel like I can do whatever I want now: I can move where I want, I can travel if I feel like it. I'm a little too depressed to do that right now, but I'm aware that when I feel a little better I really want to take advantage of these new possibilities.

The rebuilding process often involves spending a lot of mental energy going over the past. Many of the women found themselves obsessively reviewing their relationships, asking themselves questions: Did my partner still love me during that last vacation? When did things start to go wrong? Should I have done something differently? How could my partner do this to me? Asking ourselves these kinds of questions helps us process our emotional responses to our breakups. After she broke up with her deceptive partner, Lily spent a lot of time trying to figure out what had really happened:

I'd think about it all of the time. How long had he been lying to me? What was he doing and who was he seeing now? Should I ever trust him again? Everything he'd ever said that seemed fishy or didn't add up was now something to obsess on. I did this for I can't remember how many months. But eventually I got sick of thinking about the past. I was ready to start moving forward. I think the obsessing allowed me to wear out the emotions I had about what happened, until I finally got to a place where I could accept the past.

Because the review process takes a lot of time and energy, it can help if we regularly give ourselves time off from thinking about breakup-related things. Thirty-five-year-old Zoë's boyfriend, Chad, was adamantly against long-distance relationships and so ended their five-year relationship last year when he took a job in another state. While trying to work through the postbreakup process, Zoë got so sick of thinking about her breakup that her friend suggested they take "breakup vacations":

Once a week, we'd do something just for fun. Sometimes we'd go out to dinner, other times we'd catch a movie or rent a video. The only rule was that for that allotted time, neither of us could mention Chad or anything related to the breakup. It was a chance to take my mind off things for a little while.

The rebuilding stage also involves reconciling that the relationship is really over. Letting go takes place gradually, usually in a "two steps forward, one step back" kind of way, rather than in a decisive moment. According to Alvin Pam and Judith Pearson in *Splitting Up*, it happens like this due to our internal ambivalence about our breakups, as we struggle with a lingering attachment we have to our ex-partners.

Once we are able to let go, we reach the settling-in stage of our breakups. We feel recentered. During this time, many women take the opportunity to look back over what has happened and revel in their accomplishments. You may begin thinking about issues such as closure on the relationship, as well as feel ready to engage in a new partnership (if you haven't already done so). Or you may take the time to enjoy living single and putting all of your energy into your own interests and pursuits. Settling in can feel like a homecoming to yourself. After so much time spent in transition, you can finally lie back and relax—or sprint toward achieving your goals and dreams.

When you're in ground zero, the settling in stage may seem far away (or like an impossibility), but you will get there. It just takes time, support, and a huge leap of faith.

How Long Is This Going to Take?

The only answer to the question "How long does the breakup process last?" is: It takes as long as it takes. Some of the women we talked to said it took months, others said it took years. It all depends on the length and nature of the relationship, the way the relationship ended, and the kind of person you are. Be patient with yourself and try to learn the difference between giving yourself time for recuperation and reflection and becoming stuck in a pattern that doesn't allow for growth.

Judith McDaniel writes about a woman who spent seventeen years breaking up with the same woman:

> Why, I asked? What was so hard? "I kept trying to figure out why this was happening," she told me, "and what my part in it was. So I wouldn't do it again. I thought there was no point going to another person and doing the same thing wrong again." Well, yes and no. There is a law of diminishing returns, a time when the learning might be more effective in another context. Hanging in there to work on it can be a virtue, or it can be useless. (234)

At the ground zero stage, you can be assured that you need more time to grieve. But if, after some time passes, you begin to wonder if you're just getting stuck in the past, check in with your trusted friends or a professional therapist to get some other perspectives.

We asked the women we interviewed how long they thought a breakup takes. Denise had already put ten months into the process and couldn't help but think that she will be working through her breakup for a long while to come. After enjoying ten good years with her lover, she knew that no pat formula could let her know when she will recover:

Some people have told me it takes half the length of your relationship. The lengths of time people told me were all over the board, but certainly not weeks and months—they're talking years.

When Renee heard what friends had told Denise, she only half-teasingly responded, "I'm not taking seven years to get over this!" The fact is (thankfully), every woman is different, and there is no magical equation that can tell us how long our individual breakup process is going to take.

If it seems unbearable not to know when your life will be completely healed from this experience, it may help to keep in mind what Lynn has discovered in the turbulent and all-consuming breakup of her eighteen-month relationship. She left her lover, Brit, three months ago when she discovered that Brit was secretly dating one of their mutual friends. Since then, twenty-eight-year-old Lynn has been caught up in a whirlwind of emotions, though she still has perspective on the big picture: "The only thing that keeps me going is the idea that life can happen while the process is happening." Your breakup isn't happening in a vacuum. Your life will continue. You'll have good days and bad. It takes time to recover from a breakup, but the entire period is not unrelenting pain and suffering.

As we move through the healing process, it can be tempting to attach ourselves to those postbreakup emotional breathers and ditch all this "growth experience" business. Dealing with a breakup is hard work. However, if we deny our true feelings and try to cover them up, they will eventually rear their ugly head. Twenty-six-year-old Wendy talked about how denial proved not to be her friend after her breakup six months ago:

Every night I'd rent movies and watch them to keep my mind off things. Everyone at the video store knew my account number by heart. Then one day, after months of keeping myself too preoccupied to actively think about my breakup, I just cracked. Nothing happened to cause it, it was just like it'd been all built up and I couldn't hold it back anymore. I was like a dam that had sprung a leak. I think it was harder than if I'd dealt with things all along. I felt like I had to start all over again, even though months had passed since we broke up.

What Makes This Even Harder

Issues from your past, problems specific to your relationship, and the causes of your breakup can complicate the process of getting over it. Even if you and your partner mutually decided to end your romantic relationship and left each other on good terms, your breakup still results in the loss of an identity, the failure of something you once hoped could work, the difficulty of shifting gears and heading in a new direction. Thirty-one-year-old Miranda talked about how the ending of a relationship doesn't mean the ending of feelings about the other person or the relationship itself:

When you're with somebody and you think you're going to be with them forever, or at least a really, really long time, then you think of your life in a certain way. And then when it doesn't happen, it doesn't mean that all of those feelings are suddenly gone or that all of those ideas about your future simply disappear.

The loss of your vision of the future can be one of the most frightening experiences of ground zero. It can be difficult to imagine that there will be a time when you've developed an entirely new vision of your future—one that you may come to prefer.

The end of a relationship can feel like a failure. When you've committed your time and energy to another person, ending your relationship can feel like giving up, even if you've tried everything possible to salvage the relationship. Lucy met her partner when they were both in their early twenties and she'd invested a good deal of hope into the future of their relationship. Having her romantic expectations of the relationship fall away after they broke up seven years ago plagued her with feelings of failure early in her postbreakup experience:

When Robert and I broke up, a painful thing for me was the failure of everything we had dreamt of, all of the things we believed in so strongly. The failure of that was almost as painful or more painful than breaking up.

If you feel a sense of failure around your relationship, you may feel tempted to use it as a reason to beat up on yourself. Thirty-six-year-old Liza found herself wrestling with self-blame when her partner backed out of their two-year engagement four months ago:

I take it out on myself because it's a failure—I view it as a failure. I'm trying to come around to not looking at it that way, but to see it instead as time invested, and see what I learned from it. I'm trying to be very healthy about it. But sometimes it's just like, fuck it—I'm beat up! I can't be so rational every day.

For Liza, it felt like an uphill battle to treat herself well and not focus unrelentingly on what she perceived as her faults or mistakes she'd made in the relationship. While it's important to recognize your role in your ended relationship, tearing yourself down won't do you any good. You may find that you pick on yourself from time to time, but if it becomes an ongoing pattern, talk about it with someone you trust.

Your feelings of loss and grief might also be compounded by old issues brought up by your breakup or circumstances specific to your relationship. In *Necessary Losses*, Judith Viorst explains that an experience of loss in childhood makes us sensitive to present-day losses. When Zoë's partner left the state and ended their relationship, it triggered feelings of abandonment from her childhood:

Seeing Chad pack up and walk out the door took me right back to being five years old and watching my dad leave. It was that same feeling of emptiness and hopelessnesss that I felt as a kid.

So, if you experienced abandonment, rejection, loss, or abuse as a child, your breakup may be triggering destructive thought or behavior patterns developed in the past. This can make it difficult to decipher whether you're reacting to present or past circumstances and can cloud your judgment. As a child, you were dependent on others to take care of you, making neglect or ill treatment matters of survival. If these issues are unresolved it can feel as if your survival itself is at risk when you are faced with the loss of your relationship.

This does not mean, however, that you are "damaged goods" or that you won't be able to successfully negotiate your breakup. All that this means is that you may experience your breakup more intensely than you might have expected. Everyone has issues, so try not to blame yourself for your feelings and reactions. Instead, be patient and compassionate with yourself.

Many women leave their relationships because of physical or emotional abuse. If your relationship was regularly violent or there was "just" one troubling incident, you should congratulate yourself on having the strength to get out of your relationship. Though thirty-five-year-old Indigo hadn't previously considered her relationship abusive, she sensed the possibility for trouble and ended the relationship eleven years ago as things began to escalate to a potentially dangerous situation:

I think when I saw that she was waving a gun, that's when I literally knew it was over. We were together about two and a half years, and the problem was that she was a terrible, terrible alcoholic. Fortunately, I think I was always a little wary of her temper, her alcoholism, her violence, so I always kept my apartment in the city. You know, I didn't really think she'd pull the trigger, but you really don't have to think that to end a relationship!

Especially in the lesbian community, domestic violence is a largely closeted issue. Judith McDaniel writes about a number of reasons for this in her book *The Lesbian Couples' Guide*. One is the myth that two women share a unique bond, one deeper and more real than those bonds between a man and a woman, and that this connection makes violence between women impossible. Another myth is that violence is the strict domain of men—men against women or men against each other. Unfortunately, these myths just don't hold—there *is* sometimes violence between women, supporting the idea that domestic violence is less of a gender thing than a power thing.

Whatever your sexual orientation, if your relationship was violent, you may need to rely even more heavily on friends and family and perhaps seek out a therapist or support group. This is especially crucial if you were the abusive one in your relationship.

Secrets and Lies

What if you find out that you've been lied to, misled, or cheated on? The discovery may leave you feeling anything from betrayed to humiliated. Your sense of trust in others and in your own perceptions may be shaken. You may still be in love with your ex-partner (love doesn't necessarily go away overnight), causing you to hope that everything was just a big misunderstanding, that there must be a reasonable explanation that can make everything go back to the way it was before. It's easy to obsess on "signs" that you failed to notice or take seriously. Your feelings regarding the *way* the relationship ended may complicate your working through the postbreakup process.

When Sarah found her partner having sex with another man, she was initially unsure about how to behave. Even four years later, her breakup still brings up strong feelings for her and some surprise at her reactions at the time. Sarah talked about discovering her partner's infidelity:

One night I had gone out while he went out drinking with a friend, someone who was living with us at the time. And, at four in the morning, he still wasn't in bed—but I could hear him in the house. I woke up, and I felt bad. I felt like maybe he and our friend were sitting out in the living room because he didn't want to wake me up by coming to bed. So, I went out in the living room to invite him to come to bed, and I found them having sex on the couch. In the living room—my living room, on my futon.

I freaked and I sort of snuck back to my room and I didn't know what to do. I sort of started giggling to myself because I was so shocked. In retrospect, I wish I'd have just turned on the light and started screaming! But I was so surprised and I also thought, "Oh my god, this means something really significant, I'd better think about it before I do anything about it." And I also wanted to let him tell me what had happened.

He never confessed it. A week had gone by, and he still hadn't confessed it, and I felt really strange. So I confronted him about it, and we talked and fought and cried. And I thought, "Well, maybe he needs the freedom, but he still loves me." So I stayed for another week, and then told a friend of mine. She said "What are you doing? Why are you with this person? He did this to you, you're with a person you can't

*trust. Think about what you're doing." And that's what it took for me
to move out.*

Many of the women we talked to whose relationships ended in
lies or betrayal found that they simply didn't act the way they'd
always thought they would in that situation. Some were just utterly
bewildered at first, and others found themselves much more tolerant
than they'd ever imagined they would be. Lily still looks back in surprise at her behavior when she was actually faced with losing her
partner:

*I'd always thought, "If he did something like that to me, I'd be out the
door, no need for discussion." I even kind of looked down on women
who stayed with partners who lied to or cheated on them. But when I
found a letter he'd written to another woman, I was so stunned, so
terrified, even though I'd been suspicious for quite some time, that I
wasn't ready to give up on our relationship that easily. He was kind of
shocked that I was even willing to talk about the possibility of working
it out, because he knew me, knew what I thought about lying. But
nothing had prepared me for what it would be like when it was my
relationship on the line. Eventually I did come to my senses and realized
that I couldn't be with someone I no longer trusted. But it took me
about six months before I could give up the possibility of us getting
back together and feel okay about that.*

It's hard to control our responses when we feel betrayed by
someone we love. There's no way any of us can really prepare for
such an event. The most important thing when we're faced with a
breech of trust is to respect our emotional reactions, whatever they
were. By cutting ourselves some slack we can prevent self-blame
from holding us back.

You may ask yourself again and again, "Why didn't I see it
coming?" Or maybe you realize that you *had* seen it coming, but you
wouldn't let yourself believe it. Why is this experience so common?
According to author Diane Vaughan, it all has to do with where
we're coming from. Everything we know about our lives is based on
a certain framework we've built based on our experiences. This
framework tells us who our friends and enemies are, how we feel
about people and things, and what we think we know to be true; it
filters what we see and how we understand our lives. We become
comfortable in this frame of reference, naturally depending on it to
help us understand new information. The trouble is, we can get so
comfortable in our frameworks that we don't see things that

contradict it. So, if our framework tells us that our partners are utterly devoted and would never deceive us, any evidence to the contrary can very easily be disregarded. It's only when we finally get an undeniable piece of evidence that we can actually begin to acknowledge the truth.

Sarah felt completely duped by her frame of reference, which caused her to disregard things when she had evidence to the contrary:

I'd known him for years before we got together and knew that he'd been unfaithful in his previous relationships. But he seemed to be ready for monogamy with me and explained away his past infidelities by insisting that his other lovers had affairs of their own.

The infidelities in our relationship made me feel like a fool. Like one of those wretched people who doesn't have the ego strength to lift themselves out of the mire. Especially since I felt like I should have known, from the very beginning, that that was what I was in for.

Even if you feel betrayed by your frame of reference, try to remember that depending on a framework like this isn't "wrong" or "dumb," but simply human. It's the way we're designed to understand our worlds. Lily, who feels that her unquestioning trust made it easy for her partner to lie to her, now looks on the experience as an eye-opener:

I really beat myself up for a while, blaming myself for not seeing things that should have been obvious—that I knew didn't add up even at the time. But eventually I realized that I was just wasting energy beating myself up, and I decided to move on and try to use that experience to protect myself in the future.

If you were the one caught in a lie, you may feel guilt-ridden or confused about your own behavior. Sarah said:

I did cheat on my ex. At first I felt I was justified—all those "there's something wrong in the relationship if a partner feels the need to cheat" excuses. But really I felt like an asshole. I'd never cheated before and I begged forgiveness. It gave me a certain humility within the relationship.

Who Left Whom?

What difference does it make, when it's all said and done, whether you or your partner decided to leave the relationship? Judith McDaniel writes about how it's difficult regardless of whether you're the leaver or the leavee. In both positions, you may experience the loss of your past expectations and hopes for the relationship, as well as your life with your partner.

It often seems like the initiator of the breakup is immediately "over" the relationship, leaving the one who's left behind to wonder, "If my ex got over me so quickly, did he or she ever even love me?" or "What's wrong with me? Why is it taking me so much longer to move on with my life?" When twenty-three-year-old Clare's partner started dating someone new soon after he broke up with her two years ago, she immediately felt left behind:

He just seemed completely fine, and I was devastated. For months and months, I put all this pressure on myself to move on, date someone new, be "over" him. I couldn't figure out why he seemed okay and I felt so awful.

Author Diane Vaughan explains that the initiators of breakups have a "head start" on reconciling themselves with the end of their relationships. They start detaching and preparing themselves before the breakup itself even occurs, creating the illusion that their recovery time is shorter.

If you weren't the one who decided to break up, you might not have seen it coming. You may spend your time trying to figure out what went wrong, going over events and conversations repeatedly, trying to determine the reasons behind the breakup. While your ex may seem to be moving on, you may feel stuck in the past. It may feel as if you're "behind" in getting over the breakup, but your ex also went through these stages, just at an earlier time and without your knowledge.

Knowing this may seem like little consolation. It's hard to be rational when you're standing amidst the rubble and your ex already seems to have picked up the pieces and moved on. And as Vaughn explains, your ex-partner's ease in coping with the breakup may heighten feelings of rejection and loss. It's important to keep in mind that your ex has been making the transition out of your relationship longer than you have. Try not to gauge your progress by comparing yourself to your ex, because your experiences of the breakup are necessarily different.

If you left your partner, you may be surprised if you are experiencing an intense measure of grief. It's one thing to know it's time to move on, but actually taking the steps can be more difficult than you anticipated. Twenty-seven-year-old Julia got fed up with her partner's verbal abuse. Even though she was the one who ended their three-year relationship, it wasn't easy for Julia to get over it:

I remember Jake saying to me the night he actually moved out, "Why are you crying? This was your choice." As if just because I made the decision it didn't hurt like hell.

You may feel guilty or remorseful for the pain your ex is experiencing. Lucy says:

I did the breaking up and felt responsible for his pain in a lot of ways. I felt that I'd inflicted pure hell on him. But I also felt a great sense of relief, freedom, and excitement because suddenly my life was mine again, filled with new paths to create and pursue.

So, no matter who actually did the breaking up, you're probably facing the difficult emotions that come from ending a relationship. It can feel like a no-win situation. No matter what either of you does, both of you are likely to be hurt. There's just no easy way to break up, and no way to avoid painful feelings. Even breakups that are perfectly mutual can feel bittersweet to both partners. Whether you instigated your breakup or not, you are embarking on the beginning of your new life. To take optimal advantage of this opportunity, you must deal with your feelings about the breakup and your part in it.

While different feelings may arise from being either the leaver or the leavee, this may not have any effect on the level of your distress. Although you might assume that the partner who leaves would experience less pain, psychologist Vicki Hegelson found that this isn't necessarily true for women. While men tend to feel better if they are the leaver, Hegelson's research has shown that it doesn't seem to make as much difference in the amount of pain women feel.

In the end, it doesn't really matter who left whom, the result is the same: your relationship has ended, and now it's time to cope with your losses and move on.

The Joys of Therapy

Grieving is a healthy, natural way to process your feelings, but it's important to keep an eye on yourself to make sure you're not crossing the line between sadness and immobilizing depression. Maria talked openly about her feelings of hopelessness and despair over the breakup of her fourteen-year relationship:

I spent five months in low low low low land. I was barely keeping it together. I had a really hard time maintaining a professional appearance at work and keeping it together enough to do my job. I was crying a lot.

Forty-seven-year-old Maria was finally pulled out of her depression when she began investigating Buddhism, which she says helped her reach a stable point in her life where she could better accept and cope with change. Learning new things and searching for ways to achieve balance in life can help give hope and structure to the future when you're feeling lost.

Of course, the grief you feel at the loss of your relationship will make you feel sad, even miserable at times. But clinical depression is different. Both the professional literature and our interviews illustrated that grief has brief periods of reprieve, breathers from the pain, while depression can seem never-ending. This unrelenting feeling of flatness, sadness, and hopelessness can drive some women to the point where they just want it to end. Rachel's existing problems with depression were exacerbated when her partner left her for another woman:

I was pretty freaked out, and I did feel for a few days there that, I don't know, maybe I should get a gun and shoot myself. And then I kind of calmed down eventually. But I take antidepressants and that makes a big difference. When I called my therapist to say I was really freaking out, she said to up the dosage a little, and it made a difference. When I broke up with my last partner, twelve years ago, it didn't get any easier as time went by. A month later, it wasn't any easier. Two months later, it wasn't any easier. It didn't feel like the growth happened at all. I didn't feel any lessening of the pain for months. But I think it's partially because I do have biochemical depression and I wasn't taking anything for it then. So an event like that did completely destroy me. And now I'm taking the medicine I need to be balanced.

Rachel's experience of being mired in a seemingly endless spiral down is common for those who are depressed. If you are feeling hopeless or overwhelmed, seeking professional help can alleviate some of your pain. With the support of therapy, antidepressants, or both, you can better work your way through the postbreakup experience.

A lot of women we spoke with found that therapy can be an excellent tool in working toward self-understanding and self-actualization. The period after a breakup is a good time to start, as a therapist can help guide and support you through your grieving process, as well as help you make the most of the opportunities and possibilities that open up as your life shifts in new directions. Seeking support is a sign of strength, not weakness. Jeanette found herself struggling with depression after her breakup. She found that seeing a therapist not only lifted her depression, but helped her grow in ways she'd never thought possible:

Going to therapy has given me my life—freed me from the unrealistic expectations and unhelpful beliefs and patterns that used to rule me. I feel like I finally understand myself and my reactions and relationships to others. The barriers that used to keep me from being how I wanted to be and doing what I wanted to do are dissolving, one by one. I can really see now what was unhealthy about my relationship with my ex, and I've progressed so much from the person I was then. I don't worry anymore that I'll get into a similar relationship—I know myself too well now, and I understand what I really need from all of my relationships.

The postbreakup process can be a wonderful and dynamic opportunity for you to investigate who you are and what you really want. As Jeanette and other women we spoke to found, therapy can offer a great roadmap to the new paths you're forging.

It's All Part of the Process

There's a natural grief process that follows every significant loss, including a breakup. You've lost someone you love (or once loved), you've lost your identity as the partner of that person, and you've lost all of the dreams and expectations that you had surrounding your life with this person. All of these losses can bring up intensely painful emotions, which can feel overwhelming or unbearable at first. The power of these feelings may surprise you. Yet they are completely natural, and everyone experiences them to different degrees. Getting through the grief will allow you to grow and eventually take advantage of the many possibilities that will open up to you.

While psychologists have varying theories about the exact stages of the grief process, most agree on some common emotions. In *How to Mend a Broken Heart*, Aleta Koman identifies shock, sadness, relief, regret, guilt, anger, and longing as prominent emotions while grieving. Knowing what to expect can help you accept that your feelings are completely natural and healthy, regardless of their intensity or duration. Of course, everyone experiences emotions differently, so try not to get caught up in expectations of how you "should" feel; just take note of how you do feel, and try to accept yourself for feeling this way.

Many of the women we interviewed spoke of the good things that grieving their breakup has brought to their lives. Renee, who set aside time and space to grieve fully, eventually felt grateful for the experience:

That was the great gift of my breakup. It felt like I did a whole lifetime of grieving. Before that I had rarely cried in front of anyone else. When it was taken out of my hands, when I really had no control because the feelings were so intense, I decided to just let go and go with it. I sat my co-workers down and said, "Look. This is going to be uncomfortable. I feel terrible when I'm around someone who's crying and I can't make it better, and I apologize, but this is the way it's going to be for a while." I cried everywhere I went—elevators, cafeterias, restaurants, with friends—I cried constantly. I felt like I made up for a lifetime. And with every tear I shed, I got healthier and healthier and healthier. It was the best thing I ever did—letting myself just go.

When you allow yourself to experience your grief, you're paving the way for your own healing and growth. Twenty-seven-year-old Joy was dating a woman twenty years her senior. Four months into their relationship the woman called it off because of their age difference. After her breakup tow months ago, Joy decided to approach her grief as something healthy and in her best interest. Rather than thinking she should "get over it" or try to avoid the painful feelings, she made a conscious decision to allow herself to grieve:

I was just dumped so hard, after this four months where I got more out of that relationship than any other longer relationship I'd been in. I was really conscious of wanting to take time and grieve. I set aside ten minutes every night for crying, but it would go on for an hour or two.

Awareness that your grief is cleansing and healing, however, may not lessen the uncomfortable feelings that come along with it. Lynn talked about the irony of grieving:

When you're in that longing or grief or rage, it feels like it's going to last forever, even if you've come out of it before. It's just like, "Here I am again." It's a matter of learning to just sit in it. And almost celebrating it: "Oh, great. I'm sobbing again and I just want to die. Whoohoo! It's coming out. Agghhh!"

Having this dual reality may seem strange. Celebrating feeling horrible? While you don't have to sing the praises of grief to the mountaintops, stashing the idea in the back of your mind that grieving is your way to fully process your breakup can be a small comfort.

Longing for Connection

We all need connection to others in order to thrive. Especially if your bonds with your ex were your strongest ties to another person, it can feel terrifying to end that relationship. And because each of us originally learns about connection from our family, our experiences in childhood may very well affect how we take the loss of an important relationship.

Early on in life we learn how to connect with others by bonding with our mothers. The lessons we learn from that experience become a model for how we bond with people as adults. Because this process and the people involved are imperfect, many of us have residual issues about our connections to others based on where our needs went unmet or where we were mistreated. Many psychologists believe that as we enter into our adult relationships, we unconsciously seek relationships that repeat that early trauma so we can, as adults, try to resolve it.

This is not to say that we're doomed to repeat our childhood traumas again and again. But it can help us understand why we choose the sorts of partners we do, or why we get into similar arguments and conflicts with partner after partner. Our early childhood experiences can give us clues as to why we act and react the way we do, and the more we understand them, the less we are controlled by them.

None of this means that our experiences are written in stone or that our reactions and emotions aren't varied and individual. But keeping some of these psychological insights in mind can help each of us understand some of the strong emotions that are coming up during our unique postbreakup experiences. This knowledge also has the potential to give us some insight into our past relationships, as well as what we want in relationships to come.

Breakup First Aid

As you go through the turbulence of ground zero, you may find that you feel like a stranger to yourself. It's important to take the time to listen to yourself and see how you're really feeling. Joy offered some words of advice for women at the beginning of their breakups:

Treat yourself gently. Don't make any big decisions. Be patient with yourself. You'll lose keys, money, and time without knowing where they went. That's okay. Lean into the pain. It's not bottomless. There's no getting out of the pain, there's just getting through. And you will, eventually, that's guaranteed. Take long baths. Cry when you want to, and don't care what other people say. Be very selfish. Be with people who make you laugh, even if that leads to tears. Ask for a lot of hugs. Dress warmly. Get a dog or cat, or cuddle the ones you have. Write really awful, bitchy, irate letters to your ex and burn them, releasing those ideas to the air. Love yourself, no matter how hard that is. Compliment yourself. Write your way through the feelings. Get grief counseling. Eat well.

Do these and other nurturing things for yourself throughout your postbreakup experience. By taking care of yourself now, you're paving the way for your life to move in exciting new directions.

2

Surveying the Single You

It was looking over the ocean that I realized my life was complete and beautiful before my relationship started, and that even though a lot of aspects of myself that I hold very dear had been buried during the relationship and during the breakup, they were still a part of me.

—Erin

I felt so utterly and completely lost. I felt like a big fuck-up, like maybe I wasn't capable of being in a good relationship.

—Julia

I started to really pay attention to how I looked. Not in an obsessive, critical way, so much as I wanted to feel healthy and good. So I rode my bike a lot, walked a lot, swam a lot, and started to feel really good about my body.

—Miranda

Remember that first morning you woke up and realized you were single? You may have been confused, sitting up in bed wondering, "What happened?" or "Where am I?" Even if your breakup had been brewing for weeks, months, or even years, finding yourself single can be disorienting. You can never know exactly how it'll feel until the moment hits you—and you realize you're at ground zero.

Many of the women we spoke with agreed that this can be the most difficult period of a breakup. The relationship is over, and now it's time to assess who and where you are as a single woman. And, as you begin to evaluate what went wrong in your relationship and what exactly happened in the breakup, you'll begin the important, painful, and healing process of grieving.

Getting It All Out

You've probably experienced a variety of feelings about your breakup: shock that your relationship ended or shock at how it feels to have ended it, frustration, anger, sadness, guilt. These emotions hurt—sometimes they hurt so much you can hardly believe you'll make it through. But the plethora of emotions are actually the beginning of the healing process. As with any loss, whether it's the death of a loved one or the death of a beloved relationship, you need time to experience these waves and varieties of emotion. And though it can be immensely hard, it's the only way to go—the only way to come out the other side.

You may be surprised at how much your emotions fluctuate those first few weeks after the breakup: One minute you're leaning over the kitchen sink weeping, the next you're throwing your ex's favorite CD against the wall, and the next feeling a huge sense of relief that you've escaped the pressures and disappointments of a dying relationship. If you weren't aware that problems in your relationship were as bad as they were, the realization that the relationship is over can come as quite a shock. Miranda, who had discovered that her mother was ill just before she and her boyfriend broke up, said:

I was just kind of in my own depressed world, with my mom's health problems and things like that. I wasn't as aware of how the relationship was going as I should have been. So when he left, it just hit me like a

ton of bricks: "Oh, my god. Not only do I have to deal with all of my
own stuff, but now I have to deal with this huge thing, and I'm also
losing my support system for what I was going through originally." I
felt really betrayed in the whole thing, because I had been there for him
through a lot of stuff, and this was his turn to really be there for me,
and it wasn't going to happen.

Try not to get down on yourself if you missed the signs of the
impending breakup. Many of us work so hard on our relationships
and rely on them to such an extent that we deny evidence of trouble.
In addition, many women get so busy in their everyday lives that
they don't realize until it's too late that they've lost touch with their
partners.

Try to remember that, as hard as this grieving process can be,
it's your first step toward recovering from your breakup. After
you've worked through it, you can begin to take advantage of the
new space in your life and make some profound changes.

Getting Support

Finally letting go of your relationship can take a great deal of time
and energy and requires a lot of support. Unfortunately, friends and
family don't always step up to the plate to help out the way you wish
they would. You may find yourself in a situation in which your
friends and family never even acknowledge the pain of your
breakup, because they didn't approve of your relationship in the first
place, or because they simply don't know what to say.

If your relationship garnered family disapproval, you probably
can't expect the sort of nurturing support you need. Many bisexual
and lesbian women face this lack of support, either because they
aren't "out" to their families or because their families don't approve
of or understand the relationship. In this situation, you'll need to
depend even more upon understanding friends to help pull you
through. They can provide the nurturing that your family may be
unable to offer.

Some of the women we spoke to experienced a dearth of support because their relationships were not taken seriously. You
weren't married, the reasoning goes, therefore your relationship
wasn't really a serious or strong commitment. Your friends or family
may have had no particular problems with the relationship, but when
it comes to supporting you after the breakup, they may not even see

the need, discounting the amount of pain a nonmarital split can bring. It can be stunning to come out of a long-term committed relationship only to find your experience treated as insignificant because it wasn't a marriage. Jeanette, who ended a relationship of seven years, was surprised by her family's tepid reaction to her breakup:

I found that people didn't respond to me as if I'd had this very serious thing happen to me. My cousin had gotten a divorce about six months before my breakup with Chris. Hers was a three-year marriage—I had been with Chris long before she'd even met her husband. And I love my cousin—she needed a lot of support and I'm glad she got it. But she got all of this family support and I got none. Chris and I had broken up in November and the whole family came over for Christmas dinner, which I made, and no one asked where Chris was, even though he had been there every year for five years. They all knew that we'd broken up, but they never mentioned his name to me again.

Though you may feel hurt at this denial of your strong emotions, try not to withdraw in self-protection. If you need support from your family or friends, ask for it. People may not have realized how you're feeling, and may welcome an invitation to help once they understand your situation.

Supporting Yourself

Though your friends are a vital element in your support system, even the most loyal and understanding friends can become weary of your grief process. You may discover your friends assuming that you're over it when you feel that you have miles to go. That's okay. It's not that they don't love you or don't care. It's just that they can't really know what you're feeling, because it's your experience. Your friends can save your life and your sanity during a breakup, but they may not always be able to hold your hand through the tough times. That's why you need to make certain that you're nurturing and supporting yourself. You need to give yourself permission to feel lousy, to cry and feel weak, to feel anything at all. You also need to take care of yourself in physical ways all through the postbreakup experience. You deserve to nurture yourself the same way you would your own best friend.

Most of the time the grief process takes a lot longer than you thought it would—longer than you wish it would. Unfortunately, it just takes as long as it takes—there's no realistic way to speed it up.

As Alvin Pam and Judith Pearson explain in *Splitting Up*, those kinds of emotional bonds are not easily broken, and no amount of pushing on your part can make you get over it any faster.

Don't buy into it if other people insinuate that you "should be over it by now" or that there's something wrong with you because of how long it's taking to recoup and move on. Everyone has a different idea of how long the postbreakup process should take, and you're the best person to determine how much time you need.

But what if you are sick to death of the whole grief process? What if you have no patience for your own feelings? Clare, whose partner left their relationship of three and a half years, experienced frustration at her feelings:

I hadn't seen him for about four months. Right after his birthday he sent me this e-mail, and I was just shocked when I saw his e-mail address come up. I wasn't sure if I wanted to read it. And I was mad at myself for even reacting. Then I read it, and it was just all of this fluff, and that made me more upset. I thought, "Why is he doing this?" I was mad at him for sending it and mad at myself for reacting.

Many of the women we talked to got tired of feeling bad and felt angry or frustrated at themselves for reacting when they thought they were through with the process. But, because grief doesn't follow a linear path, it can come up when you least expect it. That's why it's so important to give yourself a break when you're suddenly freaking out about a seemingly insignificant event. Those random e-mails, discoveries of old Valentine's Day cards, or chance meetings with your ex on the street can throw you for a loop even if you thought you were absolutely over it.

Grieving is hard, but the women we spoke to who dealt with the emotions as they came up said it helped keep them from getting stuck. If you push them down, ignoring and denying them, they'll just spring up later. They refuse to be totally ignored. And you *can* get over them. Just be patient with yourself and give it time.

What Are You Afraid Of?

One of the emotions that probably hit you right away is fear. You may have felt it as you sat up in bed that first morning as a single person. Or, it may have crept in on you at night, as you slept alone in your bed for the first few times. Like any big transition, a breakup brings up a lot of uncertainty. Even if you've experienced other breakups, you've never been through this one before, with this specific set of circumstances. You may be facing a strong fear of the unknown: What's going to happen next? How will your life be now? This can be an exciting question—now anything is possible—but it can also foster a lot of unease.

A lot of women experiencing the end of a relationship are unsure whether they can make it on their own. Clare said:

We broke up just as I was getting ready to start graduate school. He was supposed to move with me, and we were going to live together and travel around the East Coast on my breaks. We had it all worked out. When he broke up two months before we were supposed to leave, I was panicked. I was scared to make such a big change—new school, new people, three thousand miles from everyone I knew—on my own.

After having a romantic partner to count on, someone you know you can lean on to a certain extent, you may wonder if you'll be able to handle the redistribution of responsibilities that now faces you. Who's going to go grocery shopping with you? Who will you call if your car breaks down? Who will you celebrate with when you get that big promotion? And the great stress that hits at this stage can make you feel even more vulnerable, especially since you don't have the support you used to get from your partner. The strain can send you right back to feeling like a scared kid on your first day of school.

When you wonder who will help you with your crises or who will celebrate your successes with you, the answer should invariably be *you*. You'll probably have other people who can help, but the primary person in your life is yourself—you're the one who can take the best care of you. But, don't be afraid to ask for help. People care about you and want to be there for you. Some might consider it an honor that you call them for help. But, if no one is available when you call, remember that you *can* handle it alone. You really are your own best friend and, if you give yourself the chance, you will come through for yourself in times of need.

Being single can also bring up fears for our physical safety. It can be unnerving to come home at night to an empty house or wake up to a strange sound in the middle of the night and have no one around for help. When thirty-year-old Hannah realized that her partner of seven years wasn't willing to make a lifetime commitment to her, she decided to call it quits. For the first time in her life, she was living all by herself. She talked about the safety issues that suddenly loomed larger in the absence of a partner or a housemate:

One of the main reasons I chose the place that I chose to move into was that it felt really safe. I didn't have a car at the time, and I would have to be on foot a lot of the time, so safety was an issue for me. My first few nights alone I thought, "Oh, what if someone breaks in?" It wasn't totally conscious, but it was always there. Even though Scott couldn't necessarily have protected me. It's just that you're told that you need a partner to protect you. And when you don't have one, that fear comes back and you have to fight it.

Barbara had been accustomed to living with a certain amount of fear and found that her increased solitude after her breakup ten years ago caused this fear to intensify:

Someone breaking in was a big fear. I'd been afraid before the breakup because we lived on the first floor, and we were lesbians. I always worried that someone was going to terrorize us. I ended up taking Model Mugging, street-fighting self-defense for women. It was a really good thing and I totally recommend it. I also looked for a safe neighborhood to move into, but money was a big consideration also. I scoped out not only the neighborhood, but also how I felt in an apartment—like, if I could escape out of it if I needed to.

Both Barbara and Hannah had concerns about their physical safety before their breakups, but these fears were exacerbated by the ending of their relationships. The situation can be complicated by the fact that many women have less money when they leave a relationship, while at the same time they often have to move. Finding a safe place to live that you can afford can be a sticky proposition.

It may lessen your fears to remember that your former partner probably couldn't have fended off an intruder anyway. He or she would probably be in much the same position you would be—scared and calling 911. Learning some form of self-defense like Barbara did can give you real tools to protect your physical well-being, as well as the confidence of knowing you can take care of yourself.

Lonely Hearts Club

As you find yourself with more alone time than you're used to, you may begin to wonder if that's just the way it's going to be from now on. You may begin to wonder if you'll ever have a partner again. Did the breakup mean that there was something wrong with you? Or, can you even stomach the notion of another relationship at this point?

What if you don't particularly like being alone, but you don't want another partner just to alleviate that discomfort?

Regardless, one of the benefits of a breakup is getting the time to enjoy our own company. Right now you may be going through such a hard time that you don't exactly enjoy spending time with yourself. But, given the space and the opportunity, you can discover the real joys of spending time alone—not having to compromise with someone else, just doing as you please. So, try not to be too afraid of solitude at this point. You might grow to love spending time alone.

Even if being alone isn't one of your primary fears right after the breakup, you probably will experience more loneliness than you'd like. Though many people experience quite a bit of loneliness when they're in a bad relationship, you can pretty much bet on spending some lonely moments—or even days—after your relationship is over. That's because you're becoming acquainted (or reacquainted) with the feeling of being single, living without that surety of seeing your partner in the near future. This sudden single status can make any moments of loneliness even more extreme, as you complicate the feelings with fear, sadness, and even shame for feeling lonely. But there's really no need to be ashamed of your feelings. Everyone has those painful lonely days, especially right after a relationship ends. Jeanette, who had moved in with her partner shortly before they broke up, said:

I remember feeling the most lonely when I was still with him, after we'd broken up but were still living together. One night I wanted to get my Christmas tree. When I got ready to go, I realized I was all by myself. So, he went with me. We picked out the tree, and I got all upset and started crying. He was taking care of me, saying, "I'll put the tree in the car" and "It's okay, honey! You're fine!" He was trying to give me this boost, or something. So, we got to the house and brought the tree upstairs. It was this huge tree and there was no way I could have gotten it up there myself. It was totally ridiculous—I don't know why I couldn't have gotten a regular tree myself. But I had to get this huge tree with him. He didn't help me decorate it, but he was with me, so I decorated it myself while he watched. It was really awful.

Holidays and familiar traditions that you used to share can forcefully bring home feelings of loneliness. When you do something alone that you always used to do with your partner, especially if it used to be a happy activity, it can emphasize the fact that your relationship is over and you're no longer coupled.

Whereas Jeanette experienced postbreakup contact with her ex as painful and alienating, sometimes not being able to see or speak to your former partner can increase your loneliness, too. If your partner needs space and refuses contact, you may find that this restriction exacerbates your feelings of isolation. Barbara ended her relationship because she'd been feeling increasingly stifled. She and her partner had an intensely close relationship, and even though she knew she needed the space in her life, the loneliness she experienced after the breakup was acute:

We had this agreement in the beginning that we wouldn't see each other for four weeks, and those four weeks were the hardest. In retrospect, it seems like it was a good thing, because it let us process things and separate. But those were intensely difficult weeks, because there were times when I would just want to talk to her—and I couldn't. It was a physical kind of withdrawal feeling. It was loneliness, but it was also simply missing that person. I mean, I'd talked to her every single day for nine years. She was a part of my everyday life, and it is like a withdrawal. I would just feel lousy. There was a definite physical element to the pain.

When you get that gnawing feeling of loneliness, it helps to remember that it's temporary. In the meantime, there are plenty of ways you can cope with feelings of isolation. Eden talked about her postbreakup experience with loneliness:

I was utterly alone when I broke up with Craig. I had just moved to Santa Cruz and I didn't have a single friend there. So it wasn't just that I was lonely for my ex-boyfriend; I was truly alone and friendless. To make matters more pathetic, my TV didn't work and I hadn't moved my stereo yet. But I did have a little radio, so every night I would turn on National Public Radio for company, and I'd drink a bottle of wine by myself. I had literally never been alone before, not like that. I was really depressed. But I think part of it was that I had to do it. I had to dive off the deep end and really process what I was going through.

Ironically, that time by myself seems magical now, like I was a superhero or something, doing this really hard thing all on my own. If I had it to do over again, I would've just tried to treasure my time alone, without any distractions. I would've read a lot and not drank so much and seen movies and gone to hear live music. It was such a rare, interesting time for me. I didn't have to be accountable to anyone.

After her breakup six years ago, Sabine also moved to an area where she didn't know anyone. She searched out new connections to help alleviate her loneliness:

I think it's really helpful to join something. Expand your social circle: volunteer, take a class, join a reading group, find an outdoor club— whatever. And do it as soon as you can before procrastination or hesitation sets in.

Twenty-four-year-old Erin talked about how she eventually transformed her loneliness into a desire for connection with people she cared about:

I coped with my loneliness by going to a healing place like the ocean or the forest. I spent a lot of time going there by myself, or sometimes with a close friend. There's something about the tranquility and expansiveness of nature that makes me see things in perspective. It was looking over the ocean that I realized my life was complete and beautiful before my relationship started, and that even though a lot of aspects of myself that I hold very dear had been buried during the relationship and during the breakup, they were still a part of me. All they needed was some nurturing.

Taking care of myself was really important. Listening to myself and my needs, learning the difference between feeling lonely and feeling empty, knowing I could fill that emptiness myself. Sometimes I needed to be with people and other times I needed to be by myself. I slowly replaced my loneliness with a desire to be in the company of other complete people.

The camaraderie and distraction of hanging out with people can help take your mind off of your loneliness and convince you that you won't be alone forever. Of course, seeing friends is not a surefire solution, and, though it can take your mind off your problems, your feelings of loneliness may come back. Or, your feelings of sorrow and pain may be so fresh early on that you have trouble sharing them with friends. You may find that, instead of providing relief and distraction, some of your outings with friends can make you feel even more alone because no one knows how you feel. Lily says:

I remember I used to go out with my friends and I'd have a great time. Then I'd say, "Good-bye!" and get in my car and start bawling immediately, as soon as I pulled away. I think it was partially because I was putting up a little bit of a front, like "I'm okay." Even if I would talk about the breakup with people, I would always say, "It's okay." And, even if I had a lot of fun, it still wasn't with him, it wasn't the same, it wasn't that specific, intimate sort of relationship where you can do anything. Also, I had drifted away from my friends a lot, so I was trying to rebuild my friendships at the same time. It was a lot of work and I was really depressed, so sometimes I just didn't feel up to it.

Even if you feel strong enough to share your feelings with friends, you may still experience the swing from one emotion to another. These sudden mood shifts are all too common when you are newly single. We try to keep up a happy front when we're with other people, or even for ourselves. But keeping up a front can be exhausting, and it keeps us from experiencing our true emotions.

Even the most carefully constructed front can't withstand the impact of a crisis or illness. When trouble hits, it can make you feel vulnerable and alone. Hannah had to learn to count on others instead of her partner:

I was driving home from a friend's house one afternoon about two months after my breakup. Suddenly my car just went dead—kaput! I was able to coast to the side of the road and stop there. I tried to start the car again, but nothing happened. After trying over and over, I just gave up and started crying. I felt so helpless and all alone because I couldn't call my ex, and who else would deal with crap like this? Finally, I walked to a corner store and called the friend whose house I'd just left. She was happy to come and wait for the tow truck with me. I felt a lot better then, but before I'd gotten up the nerve to call her, I felt really alone.

Some of the women we talked to were afraid to reach out for help because they were used to relying on only one person. Others said they were hesitant to call on friends because they felt ashamed to need help and embarrassed to be alone. Jeanette said:

I tend to try and deal with things on my own when I'm feeling my most pathetic. It's hard for me to reach out when I really need support. Over the years I'd gotten used to doing that with Chris, but he wasn't there to lean on. So I spent a lot of lonely nights crying, rather than swallowing my pride and admitting to my friends that I was so lonely.

Loneliness is one of those emotions that everyone feels at some point, but almost no one wants to admit to feeling. But we all need help at times. The key is not being afraid of asking for it. Call some-one to come over and keep you company. Make plans with friends you haven't seen for a while, perhaps friends you had neglected because of the energy you had to put into your relationship. And give yourself permission to feel lonely once in a while, recognizing that some loneliness is inevitable. After some time, you may just find that being single doesn't mean you'll always feel lonely. As Clare put it, "The summer after we broke up I really learned the distinction between being lonely and being alone."

'Round the Clock Obsession

During some of those days and nights spent alone, you may find yourself going over and over all the details of your past relationship and breakup: who did what to whom when, whose fault it was, the first moment you knew you loved your partner, the first moment you knew it was over. It can feel utterly out of your control. Clare said, "You know, you start thinking of your ex and you start crying. And you think, 'Why am I doing this *again*? I'm so sick of crying!'"

As thoughts of your ex run through your mind at any time of the day or night, you may wonder what's happening to you—have aliens stolen your brain? Thirty-year-old Sabine, who usually saw herself as cool and calm when it came to matters of the heart, was shocked to find herself obsessing about her ex after he broke off their one-year relationship:

It was such a freaky experience, because I've always been so logical, so straight and narrow. I mean, I can be emotional, but I'm a lot less dramatic than some of my friends. And so when I obsessed about this relationship, it wasn't like I was trying to do it—it just overcame me. I kept thinking, "I don't want to do this but I'm doing it anyway!" It was such a weird feeling, having to remind myself not to call him because he just rejected me when I called last time. But I wanted to call him again!

Many of the women we spoke to said they were disturbed by the unrelenting nature of their thoughts, but we found that it's actu-ally a pretty common experience.

Many of us find ourselves doing strange things, things we may not have thought were in our characters. Sarah never thought she was one to pine, but she surprised herself after the breakup of her five-year relationship:

I would drive by his house and see if the light was on in his window. One night I was really flipped out—I don't know what was wrong with me—and I actually threw a pebble at his window. He brought me inside and we cried—he was actually very sweet about it. I was really very strong and reserved in that relationship, and so for me it was this big release, saying, "This is how much I loved you. I would actually go to this point, this desperate point," which is something I had always felt sort of uncomfortable doing. And that was hard.

If you stop and think about it, this uncharacteristic behavior really isn't surprising. Breaking up a significant relationship is traumatic, so of course you would do things that seem a little out of character. You *are* out of character. The person you were within the relationship is, in some ways, gone. You're different now. Even if your relationship was an unhappy or unhealthy one, you may still have the urge to hold on to the familiar. People feel more comfortable with what they know, so it's natural that sometimes you may feel a very strong urge to contact your ex.

Instead of feeling vulnerable to the unpredictability of your obsessive moments, you might want to get some control over your runaway thoughts by planning periods of obsession. A few of the women we talked to pointed out that it can be helpful to try to postpone obsessive examination of the relationship for a specific time in the day or evening. Even if you're not feeling particularly sad, you may want to indulge in a little wallowing during your appointed time to work out any unresolved feelings that might be there, just below the surface. Clare said:

It was in the back of my mind all of the time, but I was afraid to really think about what went wrong. It just started building up, getting in the way of everything else. One morning I woke up at about five o'clock and I couldn't get back to sleep. So I started giving myself a half hour every night to just obsess and write in my journal: Should I have done this? Would it have helped to do that? When did things start to go wrong?

Even though it may feel strange at first, sometimes pushing yourself to process a particular emotion can release pent-up feelings. You can draw a bath, light some candles, and just cry yourself out, or rage to the bathroom wall. Or, you can arrange items around you that remind you of your ex, and let your emotions wash over you. Music that reminds you of your ex or your breakup can really help. Jeanette said, "I think repeat buttons on CD players are a whole new technological way to wallow." Use anything that is evocative and accessible to you, things that you can easily put away when your wallow is through. If you try the planned wallow, you may want to make plans or a phone date with a friend soon afterward so you don't get sucked in to negativity.

Getting Down on Yourself

It's common for us to feel bad about ourselves as a result of our breakup. Whether we feel rejected or humiliated, or see ourselves as having failed at something important, the ending of our relationship can eat away at our feelings of self-esteem.

Sixty-year-old Joan and her partner Carl spent eleven years together, and he played an integral part in the raising of her two children. Things were rocky for the last few years she and Carl were together, but Joan worked hard—both for herself and her children—to save her failing relationship. When she finally got fed up with her partner's infidelities, she broke it off fifteen years ago, but not before she'd done some damage to her self-respect: "It was humiliating to think of what my children saw—how I accepted so much mental abuse from a boyfriend who cheated on me while I still tried to work it out."

Miranda and her partner moved in together after dating for only a few months, partially because of logistical reasons. The speed at which things happened whisked her along, but when he ended their four-and-a-half-year relationship, she got down on herself for not listening to her instincts from the very beginning:

I knew all along, from the beginning of the relationship. Somewhere inside me I knew that the relationship was not right, that it would not last. It was humiliating that I didn't pay attention to that in myself. It was like, "Why was I so stupid? Why didn't I take those feelings as warnings and be the one to cut it off, or to move on. Why did I have to wait for him to reject me?"

Taking too much responsibility for the end of the relationship or blaming ourselves for not getting out sooner can give you an explanation for the pain you're feeling—*you* screwed up, so you can prevent it from happening next time. It's a pretty common way to try and cope with a breakup, but this strategy actually does more harm than good. It may reassure you in the short term, but in the long run it can make you feel as though there is something fundamentally wrong with you. If you're falling into this trap, try to get a new perspective on the situation, focusing on the inadequacies of the partnership rather than solely on your faults or your partner's.

The same thing goes if you're sitting around feeling like a big failure because your relationship ended. Diane Vaughan found that many women feel like they've failed a major test of adulthood—the ability to succeed in a relationship—when they break up with their partners. Julia had been questioning if she really wanted to be with her partner for quite some time, but when she actually broke up with him, her feelings of failure surprised her:

When Jake and I broke up, I felt this enormous sense of failure and at first I couldn't figure out why. But then I would be bombarded with the memories of everything we'd planned, things we'd talked about doing— and it was all gone. I felt so utterly and completely lost. I felt like a big fuck-up, like maybe I wasn't capable of being in a good relationship.

D. Merilee Clunis and G. Dorsey Green, authors of *Lesbian Couples*, suspect that one of the reasons many of us experience this sense of failure is that we're inundated with the idea that a relationship should last forever. So we heap blame on ourselves for not being able to "make it work," for not choosing correctly, or for not being the perfect partner.

In *Facing 30* Lauren Dockett and Kristin Beck write about how this myth that love always lasts "forever" is starting to fall apart:

Two people find each other in the midst of adversity; they triumph over said adversity; they kiss the mightiest of kisses and make their way into a blissful forever.... But the older we get, the more practiced in love we become, the more evening news we watch, and the more "perfect" relationships fall apart, the more these fairy tales crash and burn. (79)

So, if we see from our own experience as well as others that love doesn't always last forever, why do we blame ourselves and focus on where we went wrong? Lily shared her theory:

I think it gives us a perverse sense of control to blame ourselves. It somehow feels like if I can locate the mistake I made—not trusting my instincts in my case—I can ensure that I won't make the same mistake twice. And then no one can hurt me that way again.

Getting answers and feeling more in control become very important after a breakup, when our lives seem so chaotic. But the humiliation of feeling like we should have gotten out of a relationship earlier or done something differently to save it can be painful, outweighing any benefits we may get from feeling more in control.

Your Body, Your Newly Single Self

Many of us already have some problems accepting and loving our physical selves, thanks to all the societal focus on women's bodies. So it's no wonder that when we go through a breakup, our body image is affected. Some of us judge our bodies in the light of insecurities brought on by our breakups. Others focus on how different our bodies are now from the way they were when we entered our relationship. And still others worry about how our bodies will be perceived by potential new lovers.

Our emotions often show up in physical forms, whether it's dramatic weight gain or loss, dark circles under our eyes, or a happy skip to our step. Liza struggled with body insecurities as she moved through the extreme emotions of ground zero:

My body image was shot to shit. After the breakup I lost thirty pounds in three weeks because I was devastated over the relationship and devastated that he was this suicidal maniac now and about what had I done to him, that kind of thing.

Hannah experienced the postbreakup changes to her body as symbolic of her feelings of helplessness:

I moved out and I was really upset (though denying it) and I lost a lot of weight. Then I got the stomach flu and lost even more weight. And I would go into my bathroom and see myself naked, and I was really skinny, my ribs were sticking out and stuff, and I felt really sickly and weak. Looking at my body made me feel weak—like I couldn't take care of myself. It represented my failings—I should be able to eat, I should be over this. I felt pathetic.

Sometimes we see natural changes in our bodies through the lens of our breakup, distorting reality. Because of our society's emphasis on youthfulness, many of us coming out of long-term relationships find ourselves aging faster than we seemed to in the comfort of our relationship. Sarah felt like her body was falling apart after her breakup:

I think I had some sort of hormonal freakout when my relationship ended, because my hair went straight, my skin dried out. And then the braces that had been holding my two teeth together broke, so my teeth spread apart. And then my knee went out! All of this in three months!

Bobby and I used to work out all the time, and when the relationship ended I kept running a lot. But then I eventually had to stop because of tendinitis in my knee. And now I have all these wrinkles I didn't have then. My body actually has changed in the last few years in perceptible ways, and it hadn't seemed to change the whole time I was with him. So that was bizarre—and hard.

When life feels like it's out of control and changing too fast, it can affect our perceptions about our bodies. If you find yourself thinking that you don't even know your body anymore, that it's become some sort of alien thing in which you just happen to reside, you might want to take some time to stop and really consider it as objectively as you can. Is it really that different? Are the changes actually the result of your breakup, or would they have happened anyway?

Many of the women we spoke to mentioned that the prospect of new lovers added to their postbreakup body anxiety. Clare said:

Towards the end of our relationship I was feeling really bad about my body. I wasn't exercising, I felt sluggish, and I just didn't feel sexy. After we broke up I was even more conscious of it, because I'd have to start dating again. So, that summer I started going to the gym more, and generally taking better care of myself.

Exercise and self-nurturing can do wonders for feelings of grief, providing an emotional and physical release, as well as an opportunity to express love and caring for ourselves.

Many women use the time after a breakup to explore casual sexual encounters. For some, this can boost positive feelings about our bodies by enjoying them sexually and getting validation from new lovers. But sometimes sex can serve to cover up a lack of confidence, acting only as a temporary balm. Eden left her five-year relationship nine years ago. She spoke about how her breakup affected her body image:

I lost all this weight, because being in a relationship does pack on pounds. You just eat and eat and eat. And I also felt like I had a lot to prove with other sexual relationships. I wanted to get in the sack with people really quickly, to the point where a couple of people I slept with

said at first, "You really have to slow down. What's wrong with you?"
I was just like, "C'mon. Are you going to do it with me or not? I'm
not in a relationship."
*   I think part of it was that I wanted to do it quick so that they*
wouldn't notice if I had any flaws. I wasn't confident about my body.
But I wanted to have some experiences away from me and Craig, to get
away from him incrementally. But I didn't want to have it be this really
intimate thing because I didn't want to make myself vulnerable to any
criticism. So I guess I wasn't very confident about my body, even
though I had lost weight and I felt like I looked better. But it wasn't all
bad. I was with one person who made me feel really attractive and
beautiful, and I was thinking, "I never got this with Craig."

Some of us find that we really grow into our bodies after a
breakup, feeling alive and sexy in a way that's difficult when we're in
a failing relationship. Miranda took pride in her new sense of physical freedom:

I started to really pay attention to how I looked. Not in an obsessive,
critical way, so much as I wanted to feel healthy and good. So I rode
my bike a lot, walked a lot, swam a lot, and started to feel really good
about my body.

Zoë, who'd been pretty shy about her body, took to changing
her look after her breakup and said:

I never used to wear anything that showed off my form; I think I was
scared of the attention it might bring. But after Chad left, and I was
faced with the prospect of dating, I began to wonder why I was hiding
away. I mean, I had always sort of liked my body, I was just too
threatened to show it off. After the breakup, I decided that I was
through with hiding. I started wearing cute "girl" clothes, instead of my
usual baggy sweater look. I started to really embrace my femininity—
bouncy breasts and all—and feel really good being out in the world with
my woman's body.

A Kaleidoscope of Changes

The way you see the single you changes constantly in the first
months after a breakup. You move from fear to elation, from loneliness to relief about having more of your own space. You may feel
like a strong, independent woman one day, and like a helpless little

girl the next. You may see your body as neglected and weak for a while, and then you may see it as strong and able. That's okay. That's the way it feels to grow.

Your new life is in the seedling stage, just emerging from the soil. You may feel as hunched and tender as a brand-new sprout, feeling things as if for the first time. Protect and nurture yourself the best way you know how during this transition. You're laying the groundwork to be able to take advantage of all the fantastic opportunities that lie just ahead of you.

Part II

Rebuilding

Chapter 3

Redesigning Your Identity

The very first person I need to learn how to trust again is me. That's what that crazy-making betrayal thing did. I stopped trusting myself— my intuition, my ability to choose who to trust.

—Lynn

I can't believe it in retrospect, but I'm serious, I thought about becoming a nun, a Tibetan Buddhist nun. No more sex and human interaction for me, thank you!

—Indigo

Every minute of every day was just like being two or something, when the world is so magical and you're growing developmentally, every second, in these tremendous leaps.

—Eden

The rubble begins to settle. The dust clears. The shock starts to wear away—leaving you to face the project of rebuilding your life. You've been through a big change, an event that has probably had a profound impact on the way you see yourself. You may still feel wounded and vulnerable, or you may be anxious to move on and see what new people, experiences, and possibilities await you. Both of these mindsets are common. But if you've moved past the turbulent emotional state that defines ground zero, you've arrived at an opportunity to decide just who the postbreakup you is, and who you would like her to be.

Rebuilding can seem like a daunting task. And in truth, it isn't all that easy. It's uncomfortable to be faced with so much change at once. You may struggle financially. You'll probably lose some people from your life. And you'll be faced with a new single self—someone you have to redefine and get to know, someone different from who you're used to being.

But rebuilding can also be tremendously exciting. You have the opportunity to renew every aspect of your life, if you choose. In the rebuilding process, you continue to sort through the rubble, making piles of things to keep and things to discard. Once you say good-bye to the rubble of your past relationship and haul it away, you'll have an assortment of "keepers" that you must reposition in your life. And suddenly you'll have all of this new space in which to make your life a custom fit. As you begin to cope with your feelings and acknowledge and accept the past, you'll make your way to a life brimming with new possibilities.

Going Solo

When you find yourself alone at ground zero, you know you're in for a wild ride of changing feelings. But once you enter the rebuilding stage, you come to a place in which, though you still feel things deeply, your emotions aren't quite as hectic as they were. And, if you're still going solo, you may begin to look at living single a little differently.

After ending an important relationship, many of us think of ourselves as alone simply because we find ourselves mateless. We may ponder our new single state, wondering who we are if we aren't part of a couple. Even if we're involved in new relationships, we can still be vulnerable to feelings of isolation if we've lost a relationship that felt like "everything," with a partner who seemed like "the one."

The women who had been raising kids with their ex said they felt especially alone because they'd counted on help in bringing up the children. Then they found themselves single, trying to move through their grief while still maintaining a stable home for their kids. Denise, who had adopted a child with her ex, had trouble with her new role as a single parent:

At the beginning it was really rough going. I couldn't just sit there and cry with my four-year-old—that just wasn't going to work for me or for him. And I really wanted to be there for him during that transition. I had to redefine my role, as a single parent.

A Woman Scorned

Feelings of alienation can be exacerbated if your breakup was complicated by betrayal. If you were lied to or cheated on, you may have some trouble trusting others. You may feel that if the person you felt closest to could betray you, why couldn't anyone else? This specific kind of pain can creep into your psyche, making it hard for you to bond with others and increasing your feelings of isolation. Sarah, who discovered her lover with another man, put it this way:

Even after all these years, I still go through these periods of depression that I didn't used to, and I feel much less attractive than I did before that relationship. Right after it happened, I really was immobilized. Before the relationship I was much more social and strong and outgoing than after. I became a lot more reserved and shy. I pulled my close circle of friends around me and stopped reaching out. I was really afraid of people for the first six months after the breakup. I would go to parties and forget how to talk. And that's never happened to me in my life. So that's been a really shocking thing. It's all about trusting people, and suddenly realizing that people are capable of really hurting you.

You may find yourself keeping your distance after discovering, as Sarah did, what damage other people can wreak upon you. And the more you close yourself off, the harder it can become to remember the joy that connection can bring.

Betrayal can also make you doubt your own judgment. When their fifteen-year relationship started crumbling, Renee began to suspect that her partner, Bree, was becoming involved with a friend.

Bree's denial that anything was going on started making Renee feel like the wife in the movie *Gaslight*. In the movie, the husband dims the gas lights in their home a tiny bit every day. When the wife says she thinks the lights are getting dimmer, he insists that she's just imagining it, all in an effort to drive her off the deep end. As Renee put it:

I had said to her, "Gee, it seems like lately whenever we fight, Sally is somehow involved. Is there anything I need to know?" And she'd say, "No, you're imagining it." She gaslit me. She tried to make me think I was nuts. And when it turned out that she was leaving me for Sally, it was like, "How could you do that to me?"

For many of us, the worst part of being betrayed is feeling unable to trust ourselves. Lynn, who left an eighteen-month relationship after discovering her partner's infidelity, sees the journey back to self-trust as primary to her recovery:

The very first person I need to learn how to trust again is me. That's what that crazy-making betrayal thing did. I stopped trusting myself—my intuition, my ability to choose who to trust.

It can be a hard journey back to self-trust, but it may help to try and look at the situation from a more oblique angle. Lily discovered that her partner had been seeing another woman who was part of a group of friends Lily believed he no longer had contact with. She felt the humiliation of betrayal, but came to reconcile those feelings with a positive view of herself:

I felt totally humiliated because he lied to me. I thought, "What am I, a total idiot, an oblivious fool?" Even now, telling people the whole story is very embarrassing for me, because I feel like I should have known. But I also realize that I trusted him, and I don't regret that. I like to be trusting—that's something I like about myself.

As Lily found, the feelings of self-doubt and alienation don't have to be permanent. Betrayal doesn't have to keep you from being who you want to be, as long as you can learn to reframe the experience. However, giving up the space and energy you've gained through the breakup to ponder exactly what happened may not be a wise trade. Denise, whose partner of ten years left her for a man, discovered that trying to determine the precise "truth" in the wake of a betrayal can be too consuming:

Early on I figured out that it was too much energy to expend trying to figure out her side of the story—where she was going to go, what she was doing or wasn't doing, or what she knew or didn't know. Because I found out in a short time after our breakup that I didn't know what was true anymore. She'd lied to me for so long, I can't even begin to figure it out. Anyway, I have a lot in my life that I'm not willing to flush to try and figure this out.

Experiencing the pain and anger, accepting those emotions, and moving on will allow you more freedom to build the life you want to live, without the residue of negative emotion that a relentless pursuit of the "truth" can leave.

You may be hit hard by your ex-partner's betrayal, and it can take a while until you feel that you can trust your judgment again. But, like Lily, you may want to try to see your belief in your partner as a valuable trusting quality in you, rather than as a negative attribute.

Put the Picture in a New Frame

Reframing your experience can allow you to neutralize the negative feelings, like loneliness and mistrust of others and yourself, that can make the rebuilding phase a time of fear and withdrawal rather than a time of renewal. Many of the women we talked to saw their newly single status as decidedly positive. These women experienced great feelings of loss and pain over the ending of their relationships but were able, after a period of grieving, to discover the benefits of living single. Hannah, who had never lived alone before her breakup, discovered strength in her new solitude:

That feeling of being comfortable in your own skin when you're alone is one of the best feelings you can have. Because then you never have to have that deep fear of losing someone again. It was hard for me, but I've really enjoyed living alone, and I'm so glad I discovered that.

A fear of solitude can cause you to compromise too much in order to be with another person. Forty-six-year-old Kris decided that her fear of loneliness kept her in a relationship that didn't really serve her. She is beginning to realize that the only relationship that she really *needs* is one with herself:

I think I'm moving towards not having that intense loneliness that I always lived with. I simply needed companionship. So, just to be with

Julie was enough. Just to have someone there. And to lose that was horrible. But now I'm beginning to experience feeling good when I'm alone. I mean, I've been alone a lot, but it was always muscling through—I didn't enjoy it. I think now I'm moving into being content with myself.

There's a certain freedom in discovering that you can be alone and enjoy it. This realization can overcome a lifelong fear of solitude. The perception that it's okay to be alone—that it's nothing to fear—can be one of the greatest gifts of the postbreakup process. Gaining this freedom means that you can make decisions about spending time with people based on your preferences rather than on fear.

This time of solitude can not only teach you that you have no reason to fear being alone, but that being alone can often be quite wonderful. You may move from compromising in order to stave off loneliness to relishing your time alone. In fact, most women find themselves excellent company. Jeanette said:

I used to feel so sorry for people I would see eating in a restaurant alone. I almost couldn't handle it. I just assumed they were sad and lonely. It never occurred to me that they could have been alone by choice. Then I tried it a few times and I found that I have a great time when I'm alone!

Though doing things alone may not be comfortable and fun immediately, most women find that, after they get used to it, they begin to enjoy their alone time. Maria found she enjoyed her own company so much that now she's unwilling to give it up entirely:

I was so freaked out at the prospect of being alone that that freaked me out. Coming to the realization that I couldn't conceive of myself being alone was just horrendous. I mean, I'd been in this fourteen-year relationship and before that a three-year relationship, so that was seventeen years, starting when I was around twenty. And, it struck me that I was thirty-seven and I felt like I couldn't live with myself. It was really frightening.

But a few months after that, I started enjoying being in my own space. Part of the reason that my new partner and I don't live together is that I decided that I like my alone time. To this day I feel really happy living by myself.

As you begin to rebuild, you might want to make certain you have some alone time. It will allow you the space to think and just "be," without having to consider anyone's needs but your own. Many women look forward to their time alone as a replenishing period that they wouldn't give up for the world.

When you're rebuilding your sense of who you are as a single person, try to discover things about yourself that you like, and things you like to do by yourself. Although the time after a breakup can be lonely, it can also be a chance to reframe how you think of your time alone. Your new independence could become one of your favorite side effects of the breakup.

How You Feel about You

If your self-esteem is on the fritz, you may find it difficult to enjoy your time alone. And after weathering the destruction of ground zero, it's not uncommon to arrive at the rebuilding stage feeling somewhat deflated. Maybe you've gotten to the point where you can get out of bed and eat breakfast without crying, but you still feel shaky about who you are now and where you fit in the grand scheme of things.

Betrayal can corrode whatever good feelings you had about yourself before the breakup. Not only can being betrayed make you feel alienated, but it can wreak havoc on your self-esteem. You can lose your self-confidence. You may continue to ask yourself if it was something about you that made your ex deceive you. Or you may feel that the deceit was essentially a slap in the face to you and the relationship you valued. Forty-two-year-old Anne, whose lover's sexual orientation changed after the breakup seven months ago, couldn't help wondering how much she had to do with the decision:

She thinks she's no longer gay. So, it's like, we just made love, beautiful love, last week, and now she's no longer gay? There's part of me that says, "Did I do that to her? Did I turn her off?" There are so many unanswered questions—and maybe they'll never be answered.

Forty-three-year-old Nikki was shocked when her partner confessed that she'd been having an affair while away on business, and that she'd decided to leave their relationship for the other woman. Nikki experienced her betrayal as a desecration of what she thought was a beautiful relationship:

You visualize and you try to imagine what went on behind your back. Did they go to a certain restaurant? Are they romantic? Are they in love? All those things go through your mind. You're suffering already and it's like someone just dumped a whole pile of garbage right on top of you.

You become obsessed and lose perspective about how you came to be here in the first place. And it's perfectly normal, but it makes me angry to be put in that position. To me, it doesn't show respect for me or our relationship. So I feel like, twelve years—she might as well just spit on it.

Many of us who've been betrayed find ourselves searching for evidence that the betrayal was in some ways *our* fault, if only to make sense of the deceit. But, this attempt at understanding a sometimes boggling situation can make us feel much worse about ourselves and our role in the breakup than is necessary. Try to remember that, if your partner cheated on or lied to you, he or she is the one who made the mistake, and nothing you did or didn't do could've warranted that kind of treatment.

Even without betrayal, the feelings of rejection, failure, humiliation, or devastation that a breakup can bring are enough to do a number on your self-esteem. You may feel foolish for putting up with things that you now feel you shouldn't have: your partner's obsession with work, failure to do a fair share of the housework, or cluelessness about your feelings can all come back to haunt you now, making you feel duped for putting up with it all that time. Many women feel weak and foolish for staying too long in a faltering relationship. They feel that they should've known it wouldn't work and gotten out long ago.

All in all, a breakup offers many opportunities for you to get down on yourself—you can blame, chastise, and generally condemn yourself to idiot's prison. You may try to justify all of this self-destruction, thinking it's teaching you a lesson so this sort of thing never happens to you again. But tearing yourself down only makes you feel foolish, hopeless, and alienated. Clare took on her ex's belief that it was her emotional "outbursts" during their arguments that drove him away. She found that her feelings of humiliation brought on by her self-blame effectively removed her from any family support she could've received:

I think the reason that I didn't out and out tell my family about it was because I felt stupid. Like there was something wrong with me because my relationship didn't work out.

In order to begin rebuilding the kinds of lives we want to be living after our breakups, we need to turn our attention to the way we feel about ourselves. Instead of dwelling on betrayal or mistakes we've made in our past relationships, we can try to refocus on the positive things our breakups show about us. Consider your strength to have made it this far. Think about the resiliency you must possess to have been able to come through those first few horrible days. And imagine all the other things you could do with the energy you may be expending on beating yourself up.

Though Sarah's breakup was painful and included an element of betrayal, she's been able to refocus on herself—her strengths and desires—to discover who she wants to be in the future:

In some ways I felt much more free to do things that were really positive for me on an individual basis. I felt free to write a book and do other writing assignments and start to think about what I want for my life. I was able to make more individual choices, so I felt stronger in that sense. I started thinking, "Here I am, a valid, productive person, and I don't need to be in a relationship." So I think that strengthened my self-esteem.

The realization that you don't have to be in a romantic relationship to be worthwhile can be quite a boon to your self-esteem, providing a more permanent sense of strength and value because it's based solely on you.

Consider also the people who've rallied to support you and shown their love for you. If you're having trouble with negative feelings about yourself, look to your friends and family to boost your self-image. And remember: Whether you were the leaver or the leavee in your breakup, emerging from a faltering relationship can only be a positive step in the long run. Try to give yourself credit for the fortitude and courage it took to begin again.

What Do You See in Your Future?

When your relationship ended, it probably caused the demise of a number of plans you'd made based on being part of a couple. From how to spend the next holiday to planning for your retirement, you may be dealing with a radically changed life plan. Not only has your emotional life shifted, but you no longer have the partner you had counted on to help realize your practical plans.

Many women react to this sudden change with a powerful sense of loss. Including a romantic partner in life plans can be a symbol of the intimacy you share. Being faced with changing plans means having to reconcile the fact of that intimacy ending. It can be a painful experience to cancel those reservations, remove your partner from your video-store account, sell the home you bought together, or put your plans to have children on hold. But you can use these concrete, practical adjustments to help process your feelings about your breakup. Make the phone call to cancel your vacation plans part of a ritual of separation, taking the time to say good-bye to what could have been positive in those plans and what could have been negative in going away while your relationship was faltering. As you come to some resolution about what to do with the home you both own or waiting to have a child, remember that either of these important life commitments would've only been complicated by a relationship on the rocks.

Try again to turn your eyes toward the positive. Think about the possibilities that could fill the void where your old plans used to be. Consider taking a vacation alone or with a close friend. What are the options for the money you would've spent on the house you were going to buy together? Although there's no denying the loss and sadness some of these changed plans bring, try to remember that these changes give you the opportunity to make new plans with the sole intention of pleasing and taking care of yourself. You no longer have to make the compromises required in any partnership—you can go wherever you want and do whatever you want. So, as you bid farewell to defunct plans, remember to make some new ones just for you.

Time and Space for You

Not only are the plans you made with your ex changed by the breakup, but in some ways your whole outlook can be, too. Just as you no longer have to compromise in your long-range plans, your day-to-day life can now be more about fulfilling your needs and desires. Thirty-six-year-old Simone felt this new space keenly when she looked back on some of the ways her two-year relationship had restricted her. She'd been involved with Paul, a man she met in a meditation group, which held chastity as one of its central tenets. The leader of the group, which she now believes is a cult, granted Simone and Paul permission to date, but made them promise to keep the agreement a secret from the rest of the members. Simone found herself devoting a great deal of energy to maintaining the secrecy of their relationship so that she and her lover could remain in the group. On top of that restriction, she also had to contend with the demands of her secret partner, who felt that her time should be reserved for him exclusively:

I'm a psychologist but I don't have a private practice—I'm not doing therapy. At one point I tried to start a private practice, and he didn't want me to do it. He said he knew how I was and if I had a practice I would get so involved with my clients that I wouldn't have any energy left for him.

Many of us put a great deal of energy into maintaining a romantic relationship, taking responsibility for both our partner's and our own emotional well-being. This can swallow up a great deal of our reserves, leaving us with little for our own personal dreams and aspirations. Researcher Vicki Hegelson found that women are more likely than men to feel responsible for supporting their partners emotionally. If you're forever shouldering the emotional burden of a relationship, you probably don't have all the space and energy you need for yourself.

Your breakup has afforded you the opportunity to take the time and energy you used to spend on your relationship and invest it in yourself. Now is the time to reevaluate what you want in your life, who you want to be, and what emotional issues you'd like to address. Liza, who left a two-year relationship that ended with a broken engagement, is starting by getting her priorities in order:

Now I'm just trying to tell myself over and over, "It's all about me, it's all about me." I need to get myself back to where I'm more happy—more physically happy and mentally solid.

This constant reminder and affirmation is the first step in beginning to take care of yourself. In some ways you're giving yourself permission to use this newly available energy just for you. But affirming your right to build yourself up is a beginning. Joy, after an intense four-month relationship with an older woman, realized that rebuilding herself will be a long process, not to be achieved overnight:

I was a wreck for about a month, and then slowly I could feel myself building back up. It was like putting a puzzle back together. I had to lift up couches and look behind the refrigerator for a lot of the pieces, but every day I made significant progress.

Turning back to yourself is a vital but long-term process. You'll probably begin to feel better right away, as you begin to lavish attention on your needs and desires. But the realignment to focusing on yourself may take some time.

Many women decide that this rebuilding period is a great time to find a therapist and start working on personal issues. Now that you don't have to take care of a partner, you can begin to examine some of the things that you feel may slow you down—either emotional issues that you think got in the way of your old relationship, or things that get in the way of your everyday success. An objective person trained to listen can really help you sort out the many complicated issues that arise after a breakup. As Hannah put it:

Now you can think all of the things you didn't give yourself permission to think before because they felt threatening to the relationship. After you break up they crowd in, like "We've been waiting!"

Breakups give us more space not only for emotional and personal work but also for our professional and creative goals. And the time we spend sorting through our thoughts and feelings can help new ideas begin to bloom. As we become more and more clear about what we want and how we'd like to achieve it, our goals will come into sharp focus. We can open ourselves to new ideas for expressing our creativity (learn to paint, take theater classes, take up carpentry), or we can reclaim dreams that were set aside during the relationship. You have the opportunity to examine exactly how you want to be living, as well as the time and space to really go for it.

The Lone Body

Now that you're without your former partner, you may have noticed some changes in the way you feel about your body. You no longer have another person there to give you feedback, either positive or negative, about your form. You may, for the first time in as long as you can remember, see your body as purely yours—not reflected in someone else's eyes, and not being affirmed through someone else's pleasure. Lily felt the liberating side effects of reclaiming her body as solely hers:

For the first time in four years, I was really aware of what other people might think about my body, the way I dressed, everything. For a long time I used my partner's love and acceptance of my body to validate myself. I realized that I had to really base my feelings about myself on my own feelings, not my lover's. It was almost like starting from scratch, and at first I felt really insecure and self-conscious. Everything had to be reevaluated, and a lot changed. Like the whole thing about having to love someone to have sex with them—I don't really think that anymore. I think it's partially because now it's my body—it's not like the thing we share.

Many women find this an invigorating time in their relationship with their own body. Some women boost their feelings of strength, both emotional and physical, by exercising. Others make an effort to reaffirm that they love their body just the way it is. As Ophira Edut writes in *Adios, Barbie*, this kind of self-acceptance can be energizing: "Self-acceptance is not defeat. It's the entrance ramp to discovering our true power, which is rooted in who we are. When our bodies and identities are in tune, they reflect each other. This beautiful synchronicity hums with an energy that affects everything and everyone it touches." (xxiv)

This is a good time to discover what you think about your body. Are you comfortable with it? Do you take good care of it? What do you like best?

Your feelings about sex and your sexuality may affect how you see your body. Some women embrace their body's capacity for sexuality alone, without the potentially judgmental eyes of a partner. But many women begin to judge their own body in light of trying to find a new sexual partner. After being with one partner for three years, Anne feels the challenge of accepting her body in the dating world:

What I've noticed now that I'm single and have been looking at a lot of personal ads is that they always specify that weight should be proportional to height. So there's a feeling when I read that of "Well, I'm not good enough for that person." My options are very limited, I feel, to go out and date or try to find a partner.

It's easy to slip into self-doubt, especially if you don't necessarily meet the often unrealistic standards of beauty touted by our society. A good way to boost your defenses against self-judgment in the face of dating is to begin to tell yourself, over and over, that you are just fine the way you are. Even if you don't believe it at first, this kind of affirmation can slip into your consciousness, countering negative thoughts that may crowd in when you feel unsure of yourself.

Another good place to start in boosting your acceptance of your body is hanging out with a community that supports the way you look. Rachel, who is comfortable identifying herself as a large woman, has worked to find a community in which she feels embraced and where she can find potential love interests:

I think that it's true that there is real prejudice out there against big women. That's a reality. I don't want to dwell on it too much, but I think it's true. But I have a community, a fat women's community, and that's where I go for a lot of my social stuff and where I'd be looking for dates. At least I know that there's a community of women who will like the way I look, as opposed to just tolerating it. But it's also a limited community, and sometimes I wonder, if I step two inches out of there, will I be back in diet land?

Rachel's words reflect the difficult reality that, even if you have a positive community that lets you be whoever you are, the society at large can sometimes throw a wet blanket on any affirmation you've found. One way to combat these judgments is to focus on yourself as an individual, not simply a representative of what a woman *should* be. After all, whether a potential date finds you attractive is primarily between you and that other person. Eden ended her five-year relationship when she realized that she'd begun to outgrow it. She realized that she and her ex had gotten caught up in outmoded patterns of behavior that were limiting both of them, so she decided to break it off and move to another town to try to get her head together. She was able to do a lot of thinking about her relationship and relationships in general, and she had some definite opinions about rejection:

It's really more about compatibility than rejection. Let's say you go out and meet someone you find really attractive, but they're just not attracted to you. The way I look at it is, you haven't really been rejected—you just haven't found a compatible person. So you really don't need to take it personally, because it's less about you than it is about the compatibility of the two people involved.

As you address body issues in the rebuilding stage, try to stay focused on *you*: what you want and require from your body, what you love about your body, and what you have the power and desire to change about it. Try not to judge your body through the eyes of potential partners. Lovers come and go, but you will live with your body every day for the rest of your life. If acceptance comes from within, no one can ever take it away.

Solo Lovin'

As they rebuild, many women find themselves reawakening sexually. While ground zero often serves to stifle sexual feelings because you're operating in trauma mode, rebuilding allows a little more room and space for those feelings to reemerge.

As you begin to awaken to this desire to have sex, you may run smack into the fact that you don't feel ready to jump into the dating game (or even the land of one-night stands) yet. Issues around body image, trust, anger, and downright fatigue from dealing with your breakup may make the prospect of sex with another person unrealistic. What's a woman to do? You guessed it—masturbate.

Of course, we probably don't need to tell you that masturbation can be the postbreakup woman's best friend. And while some women see it as a lesser substitute to "real" sex or as symbolic of their solitary state, masturbation can be a way to really love and appreciate yourself. Nikki, who was in a twelve-year relationship, said:

Our sex life went through a lot of ups and downs. I felt like I really lost that sensual part of myself, because we were very different sexually. I feel that part reemerging now, but I don't feel like I'm ready to share it yet.

Who Rings Your Bell?

As we reevaluate everything in our lives during this transformative period, many of us turn our eyes to our sexual identity. Lots of us come out of relationships in which our sex lives suffered. In her three-year relationship that ended four months ago, Erin experienced criticism that cut to the core of who she was and undermined her capability to be a good partner:

I'm bisexual and she's a lesbian. It did help cause our breakup because, although she tries to be sensitive, she holds a lot of negative stereotypes about bi's and would make derogatory, off-the-cuff comments to me. She was also obsessed with the idea that I wanted to be having sex with a man, and that was really upsetting to me because it made me feel like she doubted my ability to focus or commit.

When our partners don't respect our choices and feelings, we may need to rid ourselves of any pain or self-doubt resulting from their criticisms. We all have the right to be true to our feelings and to make our own authentic sexual choices.

This freedom of sexual thought can allow us to act on impulses or feelings we've denied in the past because they were potentially threatening to the relationship. Some women give themselves the opportunity to explore a different sexual orientation than they had claimed before. Lily decided she'd like to start dating women:

During my relationship with Allen, I met this amazing woman who totally rocked my world. I'd never been open to dating women before, and just knowing her changed all of that. After Allen and I broke up, I knew that I wanted to be with women as well as men. But as time went on, I started feeling much more inclined toward women. So I think of myself as bi, but I really only want to date women, at least for now.

Barbara had been attracted to women for as long as she could remember and had identified herself as a lesbian for her entire adult life. Then, at the conclusion of her twelve-year, live-in relationship with a woman, she began to explore the attraction she occasionally had for men. After her breakup she felt the freedom to open her mind, both emotionally and politically, to dating men:

Even though I'd been a lesbian for about twelve years, I was always attracted to men. I guess I was more bisexual, but I feel like my identity at that time was as a lesbian. Not only because of sexual orientation and attraction, but it was also about a feminist identity, and how I saw the world, and who I connected with. It's just always been easier for me to connect with women than with men. Part of the reason that I hadn't been able to have a relationship with a man was that I couldn't seem to have an emotional relationship with them. There were times when I was attracted to men, but there had never been a time when I could see an emotional relationship coming out of it.

Me being attracted to men had definitely come up in our relationship, because there had been times when I had gotten crushes on both men and women. But, increasingly at the end of our relationship, I was thinking that I would like to try out being with a man.

Giving yourself the freedom to recognize sexual feelings that weren't "allowed" in the context of your relationship can be liberating. Your breakup can help you find a way to live your life in a way that is more authentic for you—not the way someone else wants you to live it.

To Swing or Not to Swing?

Now is also a time when you may choose to reexamine whether you want to be monogamous or nonmongamous, as well as how casual you want to be about sexual encounters. If you're coming out of an open relationship, in which monogamy was neither expected nor desired, you can decide if you want to continue along this route or focus on one lover at a time. If your former relationship was monogamous, you may be considering the possibility of multiple partners. Along these same lines, you now have the opportunity to decide whether you wish to continue with, or experiment in, casual sex. The question about whether to make use of your newly single status by busting loose sexually often comes up early on, when many women try on a "swinger" persona, fulfilling fantasies of single sexual freedom. For some, it can feel like they are stretching their wings after long confinement. Renee found her early sexual outreach affirming and empowering:

I remember trying to play it safe for a while, just going out with people I didn't think I'd get really attached to. I was actually very comfortable with my body, but I needed to validate myself sexually really quickly—I wanted somebody to let me know that it was going to work again. Because I'd been faithful for fifteen years, and we'd been sexual up to a week before she left me, and I needed someone to let me know that it wasn't all over. It wasn't a bad way to go. Somebody surprised me, and it led me to understand that I could trust again and I could really open up to someone again. It was healing and honest.

Enjoyable sexual encounters that don't require any sort of commitment from you can be affirming. You can share your body and enjoy someone else's, getting positive feedback about your sexuality without risking much emotionally. You might even learn new things about yourself in the process. Nikki discovered that she could be open to fierce crushes—a part of herself she hadn't recognized before:

I went to a crab feed this past weekend with my relatives. It was a very redneck, athletic, booster club kind of thing. And there was this woman there who was with a bunch of friends and they were obviously gay. And I can't believe it—I haven't stopped thinking about her. I'm not usually like that. And I didn't even meet her—I just saw her, dancing.

Lily said:

Entering into the lesbian world really made me rethink a lot of things that I'd just taken for granted in my previous relationship. Suddenly there was this element of choice about monogamy or nonmonogamy. I'm not really looking for an open relationship, but if it felt right to me with a particular person, I'd definitely consider it.

Because contemplating or engaging in casual sex may not have been something you've done before, you may reveal sides of yourself that you never knew existed, or you may find yourself taking risks you never thought you would.

Some women find the prospect of casual sex, or even of having to decide how they feel about casual sex, a little daunting. Maria, who found herself single for the first time in close to twenty years, said:

There was one woman, and I was talking with her and saying, "This is so confusing, there are four people who seem to be interested. I don't know what to do about this. I'm not into casual sex—or maybe I am, I don't know!" And she said, "Well, why don't you start with me?" It was very confusing!

If the chance to hop into bed with someone comes up, you may be delighted, but you might find yourself a little boggled, too. Some nervousness might be expected, especially if you haven't had sex with anyone except for your ex for a while. But, if you find the prospect of a roll in the hay more confusing or alarming than enticing, you might want to hold off and do some thinking about exactly what you want first.

You might really look forward to exploring the world of casual encounters after your breakup, but may discover that it's more the idea of freedom than the actual possibility of "getting some" that interests you. Barbara found the idea of having flings intriguing, but in her process of self-rediscovery, found that they didn't fit into her notion of herself:

After we broke up, I thought, "Whoohoo! I'm single now. Maybe I should have one-night stands! Maybe I'll have flings!" That's what I was ready to do. And I was looking for people. But whenever I got close to doing that with someone I would think, "Oh! No way!" Then, "Oh god, I'm going to have to realize that I'm not that kind of person, and it's so disappointing because it seems so appealing." I came close with a few people, but then I would just back off, or it wouldn't work out for some reason.

So, one of the things that the prospect of casual sex might reveal to you is that it just isn't your style. As in all the changes you've undergone after your breakup, trusting your feelings is probably the best path. If you dive into sexual encounters against your better judgment because you're lonely or because you think you should be using your freedom, you may get yourself into trouble. Twenty-nine-year-old Jordan, recovering from the rocky breakup of her one-year relationship that occurred when her partner fell for another woman, found her flings unsatisfying and even damaging:

I became sexually involved with all and sundry right away, but I mourned constantly because the sex was so terrible. I felt I would never know a lover again—only fucks.

While some women find that early casual encounters can boost their self-esteem, affirming their positive feelings about their bodies, others find that engaging in casual sex too early can rend newly mended wounds. Again, listen to your heart and pay attention to how you're feeling. If it makes you feel bad at any step along the way, you certainly don't have to continue.

When we engage sexually with another person, no matter how casually, we open ourselves up to other people's scrutiny of our bodies. This can be wonderfully affirming if your partner is appreciative and respectful. You may think that, because you're not engaged in any sort of committed relationship with a sexual partner, you won't care about his or her reactions. This may well be the case, but you might want to examine your expectations before you jump into anything. If you expect a casual fling to help you feel better about your body, you could be disappointed. Sarah said:

The idea of sleeping with other people was appealing, because I felt like I needed that—needed to feel attractive again. But I felt like I just wanted to sleep with these people, because I didn't want to deal with them having to deal with me and the way I look and my body and my feelings about it. And I was also sleeping with women, which is a lot easier for me than sleeping with men. I just feel that women are more forgiving, more understanding of what a woman's body is like. So when I slept with women, it was fine. But I had a couple of encounters with men and I did feel kind of freaked out. In fact, I slept with this one man who was like, "Don't you run? Didn't you tell me you ran?" I mean, after we had sex he said it three times!

Try to take the encounter for what it is—something you hope will be fun and relatively risk-free. If you don't have any expectations of how the encounter will make you feel (attractive, liberated, powerful), you run less risk of being disappointed.

Of course, it's entirely up to you whether you want to experiment with having one committed partner, more than one regular lover, or a variety of casual sexual encounters. Just remember to listen to that inner voice that tells you what you need and want. Rebuilding is about doing what's good for you, so examine your reasons and try to do things you really want to do and feel ready to do.

Staying Out of the Game

While some women decide to experiment with their sexuality, others decide to stay away from relationships and partnered sex for a while because they feel they need more time to heal. Indigo, whose painful breakup made her doubt her own judgment, was tempted to give up sex forever:

I can't believe it in retrospect, but I'm serious, I thought about becoming a nun, a Tibetan Buddhist nun. No more sex and human interaction for me, thank you! Because, like one friend used to say to me, "Boy, Indigo—you sure can pick 'em!" Whenever I'd talk about something that Hera had done, my friend would just say, "You picked her." And so I felt like I didn't have good judgment about people. So I just thought I'd swear off people. But eventually I decided that becoming a nun was a wee bit extreme.

Fresh out of her fifteen-year relationship, Rachel knows that emotions often play a large role in her sexual encounters, and is reluctant, in her emotionally raw state, to get sexual again:

I'm not really feeling very sexual right now because I'm so hurt. It's not even that I don't have the hormonal responses. It's more that emotionally, it's hard for me to get that vulnerable right now. But I think it will come back.

I don't know if I can really have serious sex with someone and not fall in love with them. That's kind of hard. Maybe that's why I'm afraid to be sexual right now. I don't want to play with my emotions.

If you think that getting into partnered sex could seriously disrupt any emotional equilibrium you've achieved, there's no reason not to hold off. Try to listen to your feelings and follow your needs.

You may go ahead and venture back into sexual relationships, only to discover that you're not quite ready yet. If these sexual partnerships aren't particularly satisfying, you may want to rechannel that energy into other people and interests. Forty-four-year-old Marilyn, who left her two-year relationship when the man she'd been seeing proved unwilling to make a commitment to a monogamous, long-term relationship with her, said:

Though I dated, I didn't find that passion or comfort level with other men—nothing close to what I'd experienced with the man I'd lost—and so I began looking for and finding emotional intimacy in my relationships with friends. It was as though my sexuality was being held hostage by my wayward boyfriend—he'd left me and taken my sexual passion with him. I started wondering how I could get it back. Dating other men, I'd close my eyes and pray to get back the feelings I had with my ex. But, damn it, the feelings wouldn't transfer. So I had to find my passion in other things.

It's no fun to think that our sexuality is inextricably tied up with our former partners, and we may become sexually involved with other people after our breakups in an effort to reclaim our sex lives. But, you may determine that what you need is not more sex, but more time to heal. Your sexuality is yours alone and can't be stolen away from you. You can enjoy it on your own while exploring other nurturing elements in your life. Concentrating on what you have rather than what you think you've lost can help speed the healing process.

Dashing the Daze of Romance

When a romantic relationship ends, many of us begin to scrutinize the very idea of the romantic couple, and our vision of romantic love. Those of us who were raised with traditional romantic ideals of how love should be find ourselves taking another look at those beliefs. Some of us feel as if a veil has been lifted, or that we've very suddenly had to open our eyes. Nikki recalled a similar feeling from her childhood:

It's kind of like when you're a kid and you believe in Santa Claus. Then someone tells you that Santa isn't actually real. It's like I had this image of who we were—and it wasn't so.

This unveiling can bring a lot of anger for those of us who feel we've been duped by our romantic ideals. We find that, instead of expecting a relationship with a real human being, we were taught to expect some impossible ideal. Searching for a myth can lead many of us to stay in a relationship for the wrong reasons.

Developing more realistic expectations about love and relationships might be difficult, but in doing so you can find strength—and more healthy, suitable partnerships. Lily said:

At first, giving up my romantic ideals was the hardest thing for me. I think that's why I couldn't admit to myself for a long time, probably at least six months, that we would never get back together. Even though he had lied to me and manipulated me, and I felt totally humiliated, I thought, "Maybe we'll get back together again," because then he could still be "the one." For a long time I believed that there was one soul mate for me—and he was it. Now I don't even know if our "on earth" selves were good mates, let alone our eternal souls!

Letting go of these ideas was wrenching for me. It wasn't just losing him—it was losing all of my romantic ideals. But now I'm glad I let them go, because I realize that they really didn't serve me. I settled because of them.

Trying to see both your needs and your expectations clearly can be difficult, but honest evaluations, unclouded by unrealistic hopes for a romantic relationship, can set you free to make decisions that truly serve you.

Other women say they feel almost brainwashed by the culture's romantic promises and expectations. Hannah discovered that discarding these romantic notions allowed a return to herself:

My mom really made an effort to raise me without any of that romantic stuff. She constantly challenged those romantic ideals about love and marriage—that you need someone else to complete you—trying to teach me to rely on myself and to examine my assumptions. So I just wanted to be a wild swingin' lady for most of my youth, and I was to a certain extent. Then I met Scott, and I thought I would just fool around with him, but then we fell in love. By the end of our relationship I discovered that I was expecting him to fulfill me according to those old-fashioned dreams of Prince Charming. It had crept in—it had developed. It's everywhere in the culture and it creeps in right under your skin. And all of that fantasy of happily ever after really didn't help me. I was raised to take care of myself and fulfill myself, but I forgot those lessons for a while.

Giving up your romantic ideals can make you stronger and can help you choose more realistic relationships in the future, but it can also dramatically affect how you see yourself. If you saw yourself as the "romantic" before, who are you now? A few weeks after

Elizabeth and Rebekah had a commitment ceremony, at which all of their family and friends came together to celebrate their love for each other, Rebekah informed Elizabeth that the relationship just wasn't going to work out. Thirty-six-year-old Elizabeth was stunned, as well as humiliated by how recent the ceremony had been:

I find that now, even when there are romantic moments, I tend not to trust them. I've become more cynical, which I'm not happy about. Unfortunately, it also cured me of my "forever" ideal. My parents have been married for thirty-seven years—there are no divorces in my family, except for one uncle. I truly expected to spend the rest of my life with my ex when we had our ceremony, and now I have trouble believing that any relationship will last forever. This is probably healthier, but it's also knocked a lot of the romantic out of me.

You don't necessarily have to see yourself as a cynic if you've been disabused of your romantic ideals. You can instead see it as choosing to perceive the truth in a situation rather than altering your vision to see things the way you want them to be. In the end, it's really a self-loving act to abandon expectations that distort what's really going on in a relationship.

We may experience the loss of our ideals as painful, but we're bound to be more successful relating to a real person than relating to an ideal. In rebuilding, many of us take the opportunity to clear our minds of the unrealistic expectation that our romantic relationships will be the be-all/end-all in our lives, and begin to sort out what we realistically want and expect from our future relationships. Jeanette talked about the benefits of dropping her romantic notions of her ex:

He wasn't necessarily interested in the same things that I was; though he enjoyed doing them with me, he could rarely teach me anything that excited me. Now I want someone who will amaze me intellectually. I thought at the time that giving up all of those desires was worth it just to have that one special person, to fulfill all of those ideals. It was so comfortable. But I'm so happy I let those ideals go, because they weren't really what was true—they were only what I thought was true.

As the old saying goes, "The truth will set you free." In this case the freedom we gain from giving up unrealistic expectations is the ability to perceive and pursue what we actually want and need in a partner, and the possibility of finding contentment within ourselves. Sarah now feels free to choose who she wants in her life without compromising for an ideal that doesn't serve her:

I feel alone sometimes, but I also feel like I have to make peace with that feeling because what it means is that I'm not going to compromise myself the way I used to. And maybe that's something else I learned from my breakup: It was good on a lot of fronts, but here's a front in which it was really bad. Now, am I going to accept that? Will I be in relationships where there is one aspect that drives me crazy, or am I just going to say "no." And I think I've learned that I'm the kind of person who's going to say "no," and you have to meet certain criteria if you're going to be with me.

Though it can feel strange to relinquish long-held romantic notions, following the truth will let you get what you really need instead of what you've been taught to expect.

Your Spiritual World

You may be surprised to discover that your breakup has changed the way you feel about religion or spirituality. But a breakup can affect anything in your life because it affects the way you see yourself. Your relationship with spirituality may change due to occurrences in the old relationship or in the breakup itself, newly evaluated aspects of your life, or the simple fact of having more time to focus on what you really want and need.

Perhaps religion played a tangible role in your breakup. Some religions make you feel that you should be partnered—or, more specifically, married, and many religious organizations do not support lesbian relationships or heterosexual domestic partnerships. Anne's lesbian relationship crumbled when her girlfriend secretly decided to join a church that was against women loving each other:

My girlfriend became a Mormon and isn't gay anymore, so that's what ended it. And it made me question my spirituality, my feelings about gods and goddesses, and all that stuff. It made me angry at organized religion.

I guess I see religion as being honest. God says in the Bible, "Be honest." And she was not honest. So, I think, "How can you join this religion yet be so deceptive?" Why would you change your whole life for something, but not practice it?

Anne felt betrayed not only by her lover, but also by religion as a whole. This betrayal forced her into a period of questioning her relationship with her own spirituality and where it fit into her life.

For others, the pain and struggle that a breakup can bring gives them the desire to nurture their spirituality as a way to understand and love themselves. Maria happened to discover a spiritual teaching that helped her put her pain of loss into a framework, allowing her to better understand her feelings on a larger scale than simply the personal:

I got some exposure to Buddhism at the same time we were breaking up. And it was just this tremendous help. I think I hadn't been open to those concepts before because I'd never felt that much pain and I hadn't had the motivation. But now I was in so much pain that I had all the motivation in the world to try and figure out what I was doing to keep centered. It was just a tremendous comfort to realize how much was my choice. Probably the most revolutionary thing for me was just to accept that impermanence was just a matter of fact.

Embracing a faith or tradition that nurtures us can help us grow and reconcile the loss we've experienced. It can be soothing to believe in something bigger than ourselves, helping us put our problems in perspective.

You may be surprised to find that these issues weigh largely on your mind. You may wonder how any benign higher power could allow you to feel such pain. Or, if you find your lifestyle being harshly judged, you may feel tempted to turn your back on organized religion or spirituality altogether. Whether you decide to embrace your spirituality or reject it, remember to do what is healthy for you. A search for meaning is essential to the healing process of a breakup, and for some of us, spirituality can enhance our search for truth. But, if the issue has become frustrating for you, feel free to put it on the shelf while you sort out more basic issues of where you would like to be next. You can come back to these questions whenever you feel strong enough to do so.

Building to Your Specifications

This time of rebuilding your postbreakup self can be heady and exciting. Eden saw it as a time to invest her energy into getting where she wanted to go in life:

I spent a whole year in Santa Cruz actively trying to figure out who I was and where I was in this world: what kind of skills I had, how smart I was, who I wanted to be around, and what kind of relationships

I was capable of having. Every minute of every day was just like being two or something, when the world is so magical and you're growing developmentally, every second, in these tremendous leaps.

Perhaps, like Eden, you're experiencing occasional moments of exhilaration during this rebuilding time. This is not to say that there won't still be moments of fear, pain, sadness, and anger. But, this is the stage where you have the strength and the energy to start looking at you. What you've experienced in your breakup has been difficult, to be sure. But it has also allowed—and probably forced—you to grow. Joy credits her breakup with helping her see the world, and herself, in a whole new way:

I'm lucky, because at least I know this kind of love exists. I always felt like maybe I wasn't a very emotional partner or person, because I'd always ended my long-term relationships without feeling much emotional impact. I never really grieved that much, but I think I just got myself into the wrong relationships. Once I had a good one, and then I was dumped, I felt so much. It was like all of a sudden I'm seeing colors and I'm having emotions that I didn't even know I could possess. So it was the best, and it's been the worst. But I wouldn't trade it. I really wouldn't.

Chapter 4

Refurbishing Your Material World

*I packed everything and said, "That's it, I'm outta here."
And then I thought, "I have this car full of stuff. Where
do I go? Where do I go?" So then I just felt lost. It felt
impossible to stay and impossible to go.*

—Nikki

*I remember getting all of Terri's things out of her room
and repainting the whole thing. It was really a good thing
to get that paint on the walls. It had a sealing effect on
the past, sealing up the walls.*

—Maria

*I wanted everything—everything that was nice. Everything
that was crappy, he got. I felt like a looter, taking
anything that wasn't shattered.*

—Clare

*I kept telling myself, "I'm not going to let her spoil this
aspect of this thing." Things that we used to do together,
I now did alone. I had a ring that she'd given me that
had a particular symbolism, and I would take it and
meditate with it, and say, "Once upon a time, this was a
symbol of love, and this is a symbol now that I can love
again."*

—Renee

When you end a relationship, it isn't just your internal world that's thrown into chaos. Your outer world is also irrevocably altered. You may be faced with having to move from the home you once shared with your lover, or you may be looking for ways to reshape the home that's now yours alone. If you combined your finances completely, or even just split housing costs and bills, you'll have to address your new financial situation.

You may have to split possessions that were mutually owned, from your home to your CD collection, making material objects a potential battleground for playing out larger issues. If you lived with your partner, you may also be faced with the sudden burden of having to complete each and every household-related task on your own.

You may find yourself wondering if the things you once shared with your ex are forever lost to you. Whether it's places you and your ex went to on vacations, favorite restaurants, pastimes you once enjoyed together, or music and movies that you shared, suddenly everything may seem connected to your ex-partner and your past relationship. On a variety of levels, you're faced with the decision to give up or reclaim things that were once important to you.

All of these negotiations of the material world are complicated by emotional pain. You may be struggling with temptations to seek retaliation or you may be trying to be as fair as possible. Whatever the situation, you're likely to find that navigating your material world may be more difficult than anticipated.

Changes on the Home Front

Whether you lived with your ex or simply spent a significant amount of time with him or her in your home, your surroundings will likely be affected by your breakup. The majority of women we spoke to had lived with their partners and so were faced with either finding new homes or readjusting to living alone in the homes they used to share. Many of those who lived separately from their partners found it necessary to make changes to their homes or move altogether because of all the memories their homes evoked. From cross-country moves to interior redecoration, most women found it important to live in a space they could reclaim as all their own.

Lily talked about the three weeks between when she and her partner broke up and when he moved out of their apartment:

It was really confusing to be with him in our space and not be together. One second I would be furious with him, and the next we'd be making out. Even though I was in shock about the breakup and pissed at him for all of his lies, I was so terrified of being alone that I let him stay while he looked for a new place.

And then when he left, all of the furniture and everything just reminded me of what we had and that it was over. It was a horribly depressing time. But it was also the only time I've ever lived completely alone, and in hindsight I appreciate that I got to just freak out—crying and ranting and then just laying there in a comatose state—all by myself. No one was watching. I could express how out of control I felt without censoring myself for anyone else.

But four months later, I'd had enough of that. I got rid of all of our furniture and moved. Partially because I couldn't afford the apartment by myself, partially because I felt like I needed to live with other people again so I would force myself to quit wallowing, and partially because I wanted to cleanse my life of everything that we'd shared and start over.

As Lily experienced, a change on the home front can sometimes be a process in and of itself. Disentangling ourselves isn't easy. Some of us stay with family or friends during this transitional time, while others demand that their ex leave their home immediately. Whatever your situation, it's important to make sure that your emotional and physical well-being is your number-one priority.

Indigo, who ended a two-year relationship with a woman who abused alcohol and refused to accept the breakup, decided that a drastic change was in order. She said:

I moved across the country. And in some ways, it was just what I needed, a fresh start. It was very hard, of course, to leave the people I loved, like my biological family. But in some ways I was glad. It was a new beginning, a new chapter in my life.

Especially when you want to cut all ties to your ex or you don't think it possible or optimal to remain connected to your former community, a long-distance move can be a way to make a clean break.

Moving can provide you with an opportunity for dramatic change—in your pastimes, your community, and your way of being with people. And while these changes can be revitalizing and healthy, it's important to determine whether you're using the move as an opportunity for growth or a way to avoid dealing with your past. Clare, who also moved across the country after her breakup, said:

When I first broke up I thought, "Oh god, this is never going to be over. This is horrible and I'm never going to get over it." But then I moved to Baltimore and I started meeting people. Some of my friends in Baltimore were more into dancing and going out, and I'd never really done that sort of stuff before. I think it was kind of good for me to go out and do that stuff. But then it was also kind of denial, too. I just wanted to do stuff all the time, because these were brand-new people and a brand-new place—they didn't know my past.

If you simply run away without resolving the past, you're more likely to repeat patterns from former relationships in your future partnerships and friendships. And if you build a new community and a new self without working to integrate your past with your present, you may find that you lose track of parts of yourself in the process.

While some women opt for a fresh start, not everyone is ready to cut all ties from their home base. It's possible to buy some time, giving yourself space (literally and figuratively) to take stock and figure out what to do next. You don't have to follow any prescribed rules. Your postbreakup experience can be of your own making. When Kris's partner of five years moved out of their apartment three years ago, Kris wanted to keep their home. But because she couldn't afford it, she had to get creative:

I couldn't afford to live there by myself. I did a lot of funny things to keep the place. I'm a good traveler, so I traveled a lot while I sublet the apartment. I had several months of not knowing where I was going to be.

After a breakup, all your material concerns can seem up in the air. Where will you live? How can you survive on one income? This kind of uncertainty can be excruciating or it can be freeing. For most women, it's a combination of both. While simultaneously feeling emotions ranging anywhere from shock to guilt to devastation, we're forced to make some important decisions about our material world. Luckily, most decisions can later be reassessed and changed, if necessary.

Nikki moved out of the house she shared with her partner of twelve years when she discovered her partner was seeing someone else. She learned that being the one to leave isn't easy, though it's sometimes the best option:

I packed everything and said, "That's it, I'm outta here." And then I thought, "I have this car full of stuff. Where do I go? Where do I go?" So then I just felt lost. It felt impossible to stay and impossible to go.

In times of crisis, it's the material world that often becomes your focus, because of the symbolism it provides. Having your possessions mingled with your partner's can be an unbearable reminder of the life once shared. During the weekends her son was at his father's, Anne spent her time at her partner Jill's house. When Anne found photos of Jill's recent and covert baptism, she realized Jill had been keeping a huge part of her life a secret. Then and there, Anne began removing herself physically from the home as she removed herself from the relationship:

I took all of my stuff out that day. I just grabbed. It was like one of those supermarket sweeps. I was just taking my stuff and trying to think of everything I wanted to get out of that house. I was crying the whole time.

Miranda was able to keep her place when her partner moved out, but she found that playing the role of "the one left behind" wasn't something she felt comfortable with:

We had this big apartment that I loved, had two cats, and the landlord even told me he would lower my rent, which is completely unheard of. When Everett left me I thought about staying there, but I realized that if I was going to do any sort of moving on from the situation, I needed to not only be away from that apartment where we had our life together, but also find my own space.

For some women, the constant reminders that staying in the same home can bring prevents them from refocusing on themselves and moving through the breakup process. Even if the place itself is special to you, you may no longer feel at ease in a space that reminds you of your past relationship. In a new home that is comfortable and nurturing, you can replenish yourself from the stresses of the breakup and of daily life.

Other women experience just the opposite, finding that their home is the one thing that is stable and comforting in their postbreakup existence. Maria's partner, Terri, wanted to sell the house they owned together and split the money, but Maria refused to give up the house that she shared with her partner of fourteen years:

We owned a house together. I was completely clear that she was moving and I was getting the house. I was going absolutely nowhere. I felt like I really needed that house. I felt like it was the last remnant of stability in my life—physical roots. I was such a mess; I knew I couldn't handle going to a new place.

When Maria refused to sell their house, the matter was dropped for a year or so, during which time neither of them spoke to each other. Finally, one day, without warning, Terri showed up at Maria's workplace with a bouquet of flowers, saying that she was finally ready to let Maria buy her out. Their experience is an example of how material matters can drag on long after the breakup.

If you want to stay in your home and can afford to, these "roots" can help you maintain some familiarity in the new landscape of your daily life. Especially if your breakup is happening from the choice or actions of your ex, you deserve to fight for your home if you so choose.

Making Your Space Your Own

If you do end up staying in the home you once shared, you may want to do some work to make it completely your own. Depending on how much money you can afford or wish to spend, this can include anything from buying new furniture, remodeling the kitchen or bathroom, hanging new things on the walls, or simply rearranging your furniture. Maria found that a little painting went a long way in reclaiming her home:

I remember getting all of Terri's things out of her room and repainting the whole thing. It was really a good thing to get that paint on the walls. It had a sealing effect on the past, sealing up the walls.

By making these kinds of changes, you are taking charge of your space and moving into your future in a positive and proactive way. The result, as Maria found, can be a great sense of healing.

When you share your life with a partner, compromise is always necessary. While Lynn did not live with her partner, she still compromised her material world for her:

She hated everything I wore. She didn't like any of my artwork. So now I'm taking things out of boxes and I'm like, "Fuck you. I'm putting this on the wall."

One benefit of breaking up is that your life is now yours to do with as you please, and this includes how you keep your home. Things that were once relegated to the background (or the closet) can now resurface and take their rightful place. Being able to reclaim your prized possessions after a breakup can help you take an important step away from your relationship and into the future. This repossession of self isn't always an easy, amicable experience, as Lynn's words show. Sometimes the struggle back to your independent self is fueled by natural feelings of pain, anger, and resentment.

Simone felt particularly wronged in her relationship. She had met her lover in a meditation group that espoused chastity, so they had to keep their relationship a secret. But, when Simone let herself into her boyfriend's apartment when he was out of town, only to find evidence that he was married and had a child, she finally understood her lover's need for secrecy. After her breakup four months ago, Simone found that her apartment reminded her too much of all the time she'd spent there with her ex. In order to make her apartment her own again, she decided to make some changes:

I was just tired of being in so much pain. Part of it was a conscious decision to do stuff and get rid of stuff and change my room around as much as I could, just to get rid of stuff that reminded me of him. And that really helped.

Once you've made your living space completely "you," it's time to do something you never would've done when your ex was around, whether it's dancing around naked to music your ex thought sounded more like noise pollution; taking a two-and-a-half-hour soak in the tub, using every last drop of hot water; or renting a bunch of sappy chick flicks or distinguished art films, a bag of your favorite chips in hand.

Once you feel like your home is all yours, consider inviting over a close friend for dinner or having a house-warming (or re-warming) party. If you're short on cash, make it something simple or turn it into a potluck. Making new memories is a surefire way to fuel your forward progress.

Divvying Up the Stuff

Many women, especially those in longer relationships, have accumulated a wide array of material possessions with their ex. Some of the women we talked to owned a house with their ex-partner. Others had acquired furniture, mementos, and household items that weren't necessarily one person's or the other's. Because the early stages of a breakup are fraught with emotions, splitting material possessions can turn in to an all-out tug of war.

Most couples in the midst of their relationship prefer to avoid suggesting they may someday split, so they rarely keep tabs on exactly who owns what. Many women are unprepared when it comes time to divvy up. Some women don't want anything that they suspect will serve as a reminder of the relationship. Others feel they should get just about everything. Still others try to split things down the middle, as fairly as possible. While the splitting of property is generally decided by law in a divorce, the law does not protect women who aren't legally married. Most women in nonmarital breakups settle up with their ex privately, though some require mediation.

We asked the women we spoke to how they divvied up their possessions when their relationships came to an end. Liza had made several moves around the country to support her partner's career before he decided to end their relationship. A lot of her feelings about the breakup were heightened while they split up their material possessions:

We were very practical about splitting stuff up. But it got to the point where I would get really bitchy about little knickknacks that he never would have had if I hadn't been there. But he still wanted them. It was like, "You can't have the tin box because you never would have had the tin box if I hadn't been there to pick it out!" He would just look at me like I had six heads and I would say, "I'm a little bitter right now."

It can be easy to use the stuff-splitting process as an outlet to express anything from resentment to retaliation to guilt. Your emotions usually hinge on how the relationship was ended. If it was a fair, honest parting of ways, you'll probably be more likely to split things in a diplomatic way. If you feel betrayed, you may be less generous when the time to split things arrives. But there are no hard-and-fast rules. It's up to you to decide how much you're going to let these emotions guide you while you're splitting up the stuff.

The decisions made during this process may greatly affect you when you start out on your own. As you split up possessions and negotiate other material-world issues with your ex, anger, vengefulness, and hurt may cloud many of your decisions. This may lead you to want to fight for everything or give in to all of your ex's demands just so you can get it over with. Since these decisions are usually made during an emotional time, it's important to get reality checks from trusted loved ones about what seems fair—both to your ex and to yourself. While Liza was used to having her necessities covered when she was with her ex, after she gave away some basic but essential items, she found herself doing without what she once took for granted:

It was easier giving and leaving. But later I found myself thinking, "Damn! I could have used that stuff!" I gave him all the dishes, never thinking that I needed dishes! I'm still taking care of him. I just know that he needs dishes, he needs silverware, and he's not going to be aware of it. So now I'm eating off paper plates.

As hard as it may be to face the truth, it may be helpful to assess what your financial situation will be on a single income before you make any agreements with your ex. If the reality is that you're going to be strapped for cash for a while, it may be worth the effort to advocate for yourself during the splitting process.

Some of the women we talked to felt that their ex-partners had been generous with them. Not surprisingly, the exes who were the most generous were the ones who had cheated or ended the relationship when their partner was still willing to try to work things out.

Clare and Lily both got the majority of the shared possessions when their relationships ended. Clare said, "He was willing to give everything up, pretty much. So, it was really easy for me." Lily, building on Clare's comment, said:

I had that same experience. But I think it's because he was guilty. He had done something wrong, and so it was like I could have whatever I wanted. As if that would somehow make up for all of the pain his lies caused me. When it came to all the stuff that he'd bought for us with his own money, like our TV and VCR, fairly expensive stuff, I was like, "Oh, of course that's mine," and he would say, "Oh yeah, that's yours."

I wanted everything—everything that was nice. Everything that was crappy, he got. I felt like a looter, taking anything that wasn't shattered.

No number of material possessions can compensate for mistreatment from a lover. But a deceptive partner's guilt can often give the person who has been deceived the upper hand in deciding who gets what.

Dividing things isn't always an all-out nightmare. If you trust your ex-partner and your relationship is still somewhat caring, you may be able to settle things in a way that feels good to both of you. Sarah's ex actually did the work for her:

He said he would pack my stuff up for me and I trusted him to be fair. When I got to my new place there was no one else there—just me and all of those boxes. I didn't go through them right away 'cause I hadn't known what he had wanted. I didn't know what to expect. But he was very generous and I felt sure that he'd given me more than he needed to—and he did. Still, to this day, I have a lot of things that we owned together, a lot of photos of him in my photo album. I just felt that I would keep those things as long as they don't hurt me too much. And that has been okay.

A couple's photo collection is packed with symbolic meaning. Some women decide that they don't want to keep any pictures, preferring not to refresh their memories of the past. Other women, such as Sarah, allow the pictures to stay in their lives as long as they don't create too much pain.

When splitting up her shared possessions, Lucy regretted having opted for single prints.

It's like, do you get doubles or singles when you develop your film? Why do you need doubles if you live together? Robert and I always got singles. He was the only person I ever got singles with. When we broke up, we split up the single set of pictures from the summer we spent in Europe. If I wanted a complete set I could always get pictures from the negatives, but I'm not going to go spend five hundred dollars and redevelop all of those negatives.

If you and your ex both want to keep photos and you only have a single set of prints, it can be difficult to decide who gets what. Lucy and Robert implemented the "you pick one, I pick one" method of splitting photos. Regardless of how you do it, it will likely be painful to revisit old times.

Once things have been divided, you may have to grieve the things that you've lost. When Nikki's relationship ended, the material loss she found most powerful was that of the house she'd put so much time and energy into over the years:

I invested so much of myself into our home, and now it's all gone. We put a lot of time and energy into remodeling that house. I mean, your heart goes into it—designing and choosing everything. And to just get in the car and drive away was the most powerful and emotional thing. That was so difficult. To drive away feels like driving away from your life.

Material possessions—especially a house—can have incredible sentimental value. When you put time and energy into something that you share with your former partner, it's not as simple as asking "who gets what." Walking away from the things that symbolize the years you've spent with your ex can be heart-wrenching. It's natural to grieve the loss of something that once meant so much to you.

While you're living with your lover, you may benefit from his or her possessions as if they were your own. After the breakup, you're constantly reminded of what you no longer have at your disposal. Miranda was especially affected by the absence of her ex-partner's CD collection:

When we broke up, he took all of his music. I owned under ten CDs. I was completely devastated musically. I'd had this huge library that was mine, basically, because I could use it anytime I wanted, and it was all gone.

When I first broke up with Everett, my mom asked me what I missed the most, and I said, "Music." So she came over and took me out shopping and bought me ten CDs.

Since then I've made it a mission to build my own music selection. I'd hated record stores. I felt completely intimidated by them. They're too big. I always feel like everybody else knows exactly what to buy. There's all these mean-looking guys sorting through things. Since then, I've been like, "Fuck that. I'm going to go in and buy whatever I want." And it's been pretty empowering to go in there and plunk down a hundred bucks or whatever and get seven or eight CDs. My collection is growing.

While splitting your resources can be emotionally taxing, over time you will be able to rebuild your own material world, confirming a sense of self-sufficiency that is far more stable in the long run.

It's about Money, Honey

Whether your lifestyle was based on an integrated two-income household; or you depended on your ex for emergency loans; or you spent all of your disposable cash treating your partner to a bargain matinee, popcorn, and a small soda, your cash flow is likely to be affected by your breakup. For some women, this can be a drastic change that forces them to significantly downsize their lifestyle.

The most immediate monetary issue that many women face is paying their rent or mortgage. Nikki and her partner had invested a huge amount of time and money into the house that they shared. Now that they've separated, they're still sharing their finances so they can continue making the payment until they're ready to decide what to do:

Since the breakup, we've both been contributing financially to this empire, or corporation, or whatever it is. But we had to—we had no other choice. And now that I've moved out of the house we have a rent on top of that, which has really put a crunch on us. We had geared our lives toward two incomes, and now, the property that we chose then will be very difficult for either of us to afford on one income.

The more financially intertwined you are with your partner, the greater the postbreakup impact. Dealing with such complicated issues during the emotional turmoil of the ground zero and rebuilding stages is not an easy task. Like Nikki, you may need to keep things going until you're in an emotional place where you can better deal with financial decisions.

But this option isn't always available. When you don't have disposable income to take up the slack and your partner isn't helping you make the transition, you need to make a quicker decision about what to do. For the first time in her life, Hannah moved into an apartment of her own after her breakup. While she enjoyed the freedom it afforded her, making ends meet was no easy task:

We didn't share money, but he had a lot more money than I had, so he would sort of subsidize me and pay for more things. Afterwards, when I was alone, money was really difficult. I was paying this big rent for the first time all by myself—it was even larger than the ones we had paid together—and I had to buy new stuff. My apartment was essentially empty. It was really scary. Also, it was hard not having a backup, knowing that, if things went wrong, there was no one to help me if I needed it. I couldn't say, "Oh, could you pay for this?" or "Could you do the rent this month?" or whatever. And even though my boyfriend would give me a hassle if that would happen, he would still do it. Now there was no one. Money issues made me feel very alone.

The sense of security that Hannah missed was something many women experience. Financial and emotional support often go side by side, and the distinctions can be blurry. Liza also felt the short-term and long-term financial impact of her breakup:

Along with our joint checking account causing trouble, there was a real loss of my sense of security. I mean all of the building for the future, and the retirement fund—everything, just gone. And it's fucking frightening.

Especially when your primary sense of support comes from one person, losing that person can be terribly unsettling. After a breakup, some women decide to rely solely on themselves in the future, while others broaden their support network to have a variety of people to turn to in times of financial need.

Renee and her partner, Bree, shared money and owned a home together. But when Bree left Renee for another woman, Bree wasn't willing to return to Renee the money she'd invested in their shared life. Renee talks about the financial devastation that forced her to take Bree to court:

I had no savings. I'd spent every dime I'd ever made on our house, on our dreams. She had just inherited over a million dollars when she left me. When we finally went to lawyers—and I'd been the one saying, "No, no, no. Let's not do lawyers. Let's go to mediation"—it was because everything we had negotiated, her new lover had convinced her to not do. All of a sudden, I wasn't getting anything. When I finally went to the lawyers, they said I could ask for everything I'd put into the mortgage. The whole time, she refused to consider settling. She tried to take away every dime of my equity. That was so creepy. It was like, "Wait a second. I'm the one who got left, who got financially savaged. I wouldn't have had to do this if you'd been fair and reasonable in the first place."

Financial battles can decimate any remaining feelings of trust and intimacy you have for an ex. And while many women, like Renee, are willing to be reasonable and fair working things out with a partner, sometimes this give-and-take isn't possible. Being financially attacked by an ex can exacerbate the pain and anger that results from the breakup itself. The court awarded Renee far more than she'd even been asking for, showing that sometimes you don't need a cooperative ex to get the compensation you deserve.

Anne was one of the few women we talked to whose breakup freed up her financial resources:

I'm finding that I have more income, because we're not going out and I'm not buying gifts. That's sad to me, but income-wise, I'm doing much better. So it's kind of a rebuilding period, actually, financially and emotionally.

Like Anne, your breakup may not have a negative impact on your finances. The money your split may save you is just another resource freed up by this cataclysmic change in your life.

The financial difficulties that resulted from Jeanette's breakup changed her sense of independence:

He moved out, so I ended up in an apartment that I couldn't afford. After a few months I had to move in with my family. I was glad that I had them to fall back on, and they were supportive, but it was really hard to give up having my own space. We'd also purchased a car together about six months before we broke up that was in my name for credit purposes, though he was going to pay the bulk of the payments. So here I was, with all of this debt, and this brand-new car that I never would have purchased had I known what was going to happen. It was so fucking scary. My family doesn't have a lot of money, so with him out of the picture I really knew that I was on my own—sink or swim.

Sometimes it's not just a matter of making a choice to cut back on spending. When you've accumulated significant debt or financial obligations, you may need to make sacrifices to stay afloat. But no matter what you have to do, whether it's living with others, filing for bankruptcy, or giving up the trip you'd so looked forward to, sometimes the pain these sacrifices bring is mixed with the satisfaction of discovering that you can survive on your own. As Jeanette discovered, the financial part of breakups can dramatically change the landscape of your life, but if you meet the challenge, you can be left with a feeling of security that you never anticipated:

The thing about it that I keep coming back to, though, is that I did it. I took care of myself—and I didn't think I could do that before. That's why I was so terrified in the beginning. But I've reached the point where I know that, no matter what, I can make this work. I mean, it was more comfortable in the relationship, and I hope to have that again someday—though I'll certainly be more cautious and maintain at least some level of independence—but the knowledge that I can do it myself is invaluable to me.

The Woman of the House

Modern couples often split household labor based on abilities (you love gardening, I have allergies) and preferences (paying the bills makes you nauseated, I love crunching numbers). But once a relationship ends, you're left to do everything on your own, including the things you hate and the things you're aren't so great at.

Jeanette found a few emotional blocks to doing certain activities. Having relied heavily on her partner to take care of the house, she remembers clearly the first time she started relying on herself:

One morning about a week into the breakup, I woke up and the house was a mess and I thought, "Okay, I'm going to clean it, I can do it by myself." Chris always took care of that stuff, and I had this mental block, like "I can't do it," even though I really could. I just felt like I couldn't. Looking back, I think it was partially my way of convincing myself that I needed him, that I couldn't leave the relationship.

When I got to the cat box, I just felt defeated. We had this practically full fifty-pound bag of kitty litter that he'd bought, and I thought, "I can't lift that thing." But I finally just did it. And I was so proud of myself. It was the first sign that I really could make it without him.

I was thinking about the kitty litter incident the other day, and I was realizing how differently I think of things now. I realized for the first time, two years later, that I didn't even have to lift the bag—I could have easily scooped it out with something smaller. But I had it in my head that I had to do it like he did it, and that I was incapable. Since then, I've really made a point of finding my own way to get things done.

In the rebuilding phase of your breakup, one of the tasks is to reassess what you're truly capable of doing. Get creative. If you're a terrible cook, take a cooking class or get a simple cookbook and try making one new dish a week to supplement your frozen dinners and cartons of takeout. If you hate mowing the lawn, hire a neighborhood kid to do it. If you love cleaning and you need some help with child care, see if your friends will swap baby-sitting hours for housecleaning. Like Jeanette, you may initially feel stuck trying to do things exactly how your ex used to do them. But doing things your own way can give you a sense of strength and independence.

Even if you didn't live with your partner, there may have been things you did for each other that you now miss. Part of the difficulty for Anne in breaking up was that undone tasks were a painful reminder that her relationship was over:

She loved to iron and I hate to iron. And I've got this shirt that needs to be ironed and it's not getting ironed. Her half of what needs to get done isn't getting done. It's not a crisis, but it's a reminder.

If you experience painful echoes when addressing household responsibilities, you can experiment to see what helps best alleviate your pain and move you toward the future. You can try doing the tasks yourself and see if that keeps uncompleted tasks from reminding you of your breakup. If it's just too painful for now and it can wait, you may also choose to just let it go.

Hannah had never felt particularly handy before her breakup. But when faced with the myriad little tasks that needed to be done in her new apartment, she took to her new role with enthusiasm:

I'd never had a toolbox before. I'd never really needed any tools because Scott usually fixed things around the house. When we split up, I realized that I couldn't count on anyone else to help me fix things, put up pictures, or put together new furniture. I had to take that responsibility. So, I went right out and bought myself a yellow toolbox and filled it with a bunch of tools and got right down to fixing everything in sight. It made me feel really strong. It also made me wonder why on earth I'd let my ex do all the handiwork in the past. I was perfectly capable of doing it myself!

Because some tasks are often split down gender role lines, you may find yourself faced with tasks that you'd never had to contemplate before. Some of these tasks can instill quite a bit of fear in the uninitiated, simply because they're so unfamiliar. Zoë was terrified to face car trouble after her breakup:

I was doing pretty well alone, feeling pretty sure of myself. Then, all of a sudden, I noticed the brake warning light flashing red. You know, the little light that warns that your brakes are about to fail, or whatever? I remember just feeling my face start to burn and my heart pounding. Car stuff just freaked me out, because it was so expensive and potentially dangerous. Also because I just knew nothing about cars. Chad had always sort of kept his eye on both of our cars, and I was happy to let him take care of it.

Well, I got a grip on myself and drove home. I really didn't want to let this car thing beat me, 'cause I'd been feeling so good. So, I sat down and thought about the problem, and I remembered that this company, Chilton, publishes car maintenance books for specific cars. So, I went to Grand Auto, where I bought a Chilton's guide. I figured out by looking at the book that my brake fluid was low, and that might be causing the light to flash. So, I bought the fluid the book recommended, put it in where the picture in the book showed me, and—voila!—the light stopped flashing! I felt so good that I'd avoided taking it into the mechanic—that I had fixed it all by myself.

Some women are only too happy to take over complete responsibility for household chores if it means a greater feeling of independence. Zoë felt liberated when faced with her new chores, because she was only cleaning up *her* mess and no longer responsible for cleaning up after someone else:

In some ways it was hard to have to do all of the work, but I actually felt relieved. I was so glad to be cleaning only my dirt, you know? I didn't have to scoop his hair out of the shower, didn't have to pick up any of his dirty underwear, didn't have to wash pans that he'd burned food on. It was all mine, and getting rid of the resentment I'd been carrying around about the unequal division of labor was such a relief. I didn't have to be mad about it anymore. And I never had to clean up after him again.

Part of establishing your very own space is discovering the right to mess it up any way you want—and being the only one responsible for cleaning it. You can't ask your partner for help, but you don't have to argue about chore distribution or clean up after anyone but yourself. Sometimes, the relief outweighs the fatigue.

What's Ours Is Mine: Reclaiming What You Used to Share

When you're in a significant relationship, especially over a long period of time, parts of your life become connected to memories of your partner. Places you shared, music you both loved, and things you did together may no longer look the same after a breakup. Suddenly, hearing "our song" on the radio brings tears or rage, rather than feelings of warmth and connectedness. The prospect of a Sunday morning at your favorite cafe—where you used to go every weekend with your ex—doesn't feel so relaxing. And just thinking about hiking on your favorite trails without your partner feels like climbing a mountain.

At first, it may be easier to listen to talk radio, drink instant coffee at home, and become a couch potato. But if the things you shared were things that you would've loved even without your partner's company, you may eventually wonder when you're going to get your life back. As you begin rebuilding your life to your own specifications, you'll have to decide how much of the past you want to use in your newly designed existence and how much you want to leave in the past.

My Place or Ours?

Whether it's their favorite local restaurant or the foreign country they lived in with an ex, many women find returning to places they once shared with their ex extremely painful, especially in the ground zero and rebuilding stages of a breakup. Because each place has its own particular combination of sights, sounds, and scents, returning can result in a sensory experience that bombards you with flashes of moments shared with your ex. This visceral, physical experience can make it hard to enjoy places you once loved. Some women decide never to return, preferring to leave it in the past. But when you love a place and want it to remain in your life, you may decide to reclaim it.

When Maria's relationship ended, she chose to reclaim the coastline that she'd once shared with her lover:

Terri and I would go to the coast, spending a lot of time there at her family's house, so at first I felt like it wasn't right for me to go. But then I just decided that I loved it, too, you know? I decided that it could be mine, too. I was recently in her hometown for a conference and, even nine years later, it was interesting how much she came to mind and how nostalgic I got. Knowing that she still had family there and that now I was a stranger in that place.

Of course, reclaiming a place does not necessarily mean that you've detached it from all memories of the past. Feelings of melancholy may coexist with your new experiences, combining to create a fuller reflection of your relationship with a place that's still meaningful to you.

Lynn's partner, Brit, lived in a cooperative community that Lynn herself had once belonged to before she met Brit. When they broke up, Brit's resident status made it hard for Lynn to visit the place that meant so much to her:

I kept trying to go back with integrity, but I couldn't do it. Finally, I was driving by, and I thought, "If it wasn't for her, there is no reason why I wouldn't stop by and say hello to people." I went there, and she wasn't there, and I walked around, and the image I'd built of her shrunk, and she became a littler, regular person.

The act of reclaiming can be an empowering one, serving as proof that you can move on without your ex. When a place is important to both partners, it may feel as if you don't have the right to revisit your old haunts. But as long as you're respecting your ex's privacy and visiting a place to nourish yourself, reclaiming can be a positive step towards rebuilding.

When the places that remind you of the past include the city you live in, reclaiming can feel like an insurmountable but essential task to taking back your everyday life. Sarah said:

My big problem, for the first little while, was that he lived ten blocks away. My other problem was every street corner in the city—we had lived here for years together. So it took me a long time to feel like the city was mine again. I would really miss him even just walking down the streets.

When you've spent a lot of time with someone you're now without, it can be hard to go about your usual routine without being constantly reminded of how things used to be. It's only with time and a conscious decision to put one foot in front of the other that you can begin to add new memories into the mix, slowly balancing out your memories of the past.

Whether it's the streets you walk everyday or the places you went to for weekend getaways, reclaiming is something that can feel different alone, with friends, or with new lovers. A year after her breakup, Jeanette found herself on a road trip with a friend. As they hit different spots that each wanted to visit, her friend mentioned wanting to go to a place that Jeanette used to share with her ex:

At first I was a little leery. But I also really loved this town, and there was a historical landmark there that my ex and I had never gotten around to going to that I really wanted to see. So I warned my friend that it might be kind of hard for me, and we decided to go ahead. While we were driving, we passed this hotel that he and I stayed at during a few of the most intense, wonderful times we'd ever spent together. And I said, "That's where we used to stay," sort of nonchalantly. And my friend, who I've known forever, said, "You okay?" And just the way she said it, I really felt her concern, and I got a little teary. Partially because of how things used to be, and partially because I was really happy with the way things were changing. Being there with her was a reminder of all the people who were still in my life who cared about me and who I loved a lot.

The support of friends can help during the first few times back to a place you want to revisit. Sarah found that it can also make a difference sharing a place with a new lover:

When I would go to these old places when I wasn't seeing somebody, it would be hard. But when I went with someone I was seeing, it felt more like I was getting there, like I was being able to have that experience on my own. His ghost wasn't necessarily there anymore. I would think about him a little bit, but then I would remind myself that this was my opportunity to get the place back for myself.

They're Playing Our Song

Hearing music can be like taking a ride in a time machine—transporting you right back to the first time you heard the song or to an important moment when that music was playing. Many couples even choose a song to symbolize their love for each other. After a breakup, those same songs can send us right back into breakup pain. The radio can become your worst enemy, playing sappy love song after love song. It may hurt to even look at your favorite CDs. Some women choose to listen to music that reminds them of their ex-lovers while they wallow through ground zero, but once you start to rebuild, wallowing every day makes it hard to move forward. Barbara found it best to put some of her favorite music away:

Music was a big one. Certain things that we'd listened to together. I just had to stop listening to those thing. Just for a while, because it was too painful. I reclaimed that music years later.

Once you've fully dealt with the aftermath of a breakup, listening to music or reminiscing about the past won't be as painful, but you may still be reminded of the past. Jeanette, whose relationship ended two years ago, said:

There's some music that can still make me feel a little melancholy. It doesn't keep me from listening to the music, but it will always be just a little connected to the past.

Hannah finds some sadness in letting go of the connection between the material world and past experiences:

Sometimes it makes me sad that you accrue these new experiences, and the meaning that you had begins to slip away, and that meaning was so important at one point. It's the romantic part of me saying, "Oh, you have these big dreams and big ideas, and then what do they mean?" In reclaiming some of my music, I want it back, but there's a part of me that's sorry to not feel that twinge of sadness when I hear the songs.

Just Passing Time

When spending time with a lover, we may share activities that we've always enjoyed or build new pastimes with our partners. After a breakup, we're are faced with the choice of which of these activities we want to continue engaging in, whether alone or with new people. Especially when there's one particular hobby that you used to do together, it can feel strange and lonely to continue it without your ex. Anne chose to avoid one significant activity altogether:

We used to go antiquing. You know, going to antique shops, that kind of thing. Now I can't do it at all, not yet, by myself. Because we shared that together, we found little treasures together. So I can't do that.

Nikki shared virtually every pastime with her partner, and felt as if nothing was the same after the breakup:

We did almost everything together. So now, even if I find a really good bottle of wine, I don't want to open it, I want to save it—'cause I know that she would appreciate it. I'm trying to start my own wine collection so that I can transfer that thing that was "our thing" to "my thing."

When you're used to sharing something with a lover, continuing it alone can be a constant reminder that the person is no longer there enjoying it with you. But as you begin to rebuild, it's important to realize that doing things that you enjoy and appreciate is important to the replenishing of your life.

Holidays and other annual events are often painful reminders of an ex's absence. Whether you celebrated with just your lover, with friends, or with family, holidays may look different now without your partner. Denise talked about how she's worked to reclaim these days for herself:

For me, the biggest reclaiming has been around events and rituals with the children. I didn't do holidays a lot when I was a kid. We did them, but they weren't particularly joyous occasions. So Mary really taught me a lot about having fun at the holidays.

It was a little rough going at first: I'd get through one, and then I'd anticipate the next one. But I think what I did was grieve the loss of her and develop some rituals for myself around the children. The hardest one, I must say, that I didn't anticipate, was Valentine's Day. I saw that one coming about three weeks away, when suddenly there were little red things in the window—and I thought, "Hearts! This could only mean that dreaded day!"

She had brought meaning to me for Valentine's Day. I hadn't cared that much about it previously. So a close friend of mine said, "Well, I guess that means that you're just going to have to send out Valentine's Day cards to all of your friends." So one day, I went to the stationery store and bought lots of really beautiful cards, and I sat down and wrote out seven cards, and made hearts for the kids' bedroom doors. When I got home Valentine's evening, there were phone messages from my friends, and I was just so loved that day. It feels like I'm reclaiming some kind of personal joy.

It can be tempting to bear down and try and "get through" a holiday. But by making something your own, celebrating with the people you love who are still a part of your life, you may discover a feeling of love and acceptance that brings joy back to the event you dreaded.

The anniversary you once shared with your lover can also be an especially painful day, reminding you of how your life used to be. You may choose to set aside this day to give yourself the space to grieve, or, as Jeanette did, you may want to put something nice in its place:

Our anniversary had been really important to us throughout our relationship. When it started to roll around that first year, I knew it wasn't going to be a fun day for me. But then I thought, hey, it's a day in my life. Why should it have to suck? So I asked my friend if I could take her out to the theater. It just happened to be the opening night for A Streetcar Named Desire. *So she paid for dinner, and I paid for the tickets, and we had a really great time.*

When things come up that you know will be painful, it can be helpful to do something new and exciting, starting new traditions or building new experiences. It can also be soothing to surround yourself with the people you care about, who can serve as reminders that you're not alone and that there are people who love and support you.

Our Past Is My Past

Perhaps one of the biggest things to reclaim after a breakup is your memories of the past. During the ground zero and rebuilding stages of a breakup, it's sometimes easier to lock away memories of the good times and the important things you shared. But as time goes by and you come to accept what has happened, you may want to begin reclaiming the past. Nikki did this in a concrete way:

I sat down and made a photo album of the entire twelve years that we were together. Starting from the very beginning and going all the way through. Dedicating special pages to her father who passed away during the relationship, the two dogs who passed away, all the vacations that we took. And that was really hard, but now I feel like I don't need to avoid that so much. It was really powerful for me to just go through it like that.

By being able to think about things you shared with your ex in the past, you can give yourself the gift of important memories.

When asked what she reclaimed after her breakup, Renee said:

Everything. I kept telling myself, "I'm not going to let her spoil this aspect of this thing." Things that we used to do together, I now did alone. I had a ring that she'd given me that had a particular symbolism, and I would take it and meditate with it, and say, "Once upon a time, this was a symbol of love, and this is a symbol now that I can love again."

There's also a point where you don't have to reclaim everything. You can't make it all up to yourself. I'd bought a home, and I was trying to find furniture, because I'd lost a lot of furniture when she left. And I found a table almost just like the coffee table we had. I got it in the car and was halfway home, and I thought, "Why am I doing this? This is a big, clunky piece. It's going to make the room darker." And then I thought, "You know, this isn't going to give me back what it was like when we first bought the coffee table together." So I turned around and brought it back and bought myself a beautiful glass coffee table that I adore and that was nothing like anything she would've ever picked out. And so I stopped trying to replace all of the things I had lost.

Reclaiming is a complicated process. It's up to you to decide what you want to reclaim and what you choose to leave behind. As you move forward in your life, you can include or exclude any places, music, activities, or memories that you choose. What's important is that you are true to your own desires and needs.

Chapter 5

Renovating Your Community

My new friendships and old friendships that have gotten stronger have been some of the best things about the breakup. I've discovered that my friends are my safety net, but it's not the same as leaning on a big crutch, like I did in my relationship.

—Hannah

When we broke up, my brother was just devastated. And I'd even thought about that, too. I was like, "Oh, my God. If I leave this engagement my brother is going to be really disappointed." It's amazing how that delayed me, even when I knew it was time to break up. And my brother was really angry at me for a while. But also, he can look at it as an example: You've got to trust your heart. But, inevitably, you're going to disappoint people.

—Shannon

I never again wanted to put all of my eggs in just one basket. I had this incredible need to develop a life that was not dependent upon one person, who could, through her actions, devastate me. So I started a lot of new relationships.

—Maria

When you and your ex parted ways, you probably also said good-bye to a few friends. You may have lost them because they were your ex's friends to begin with (so you felt you had no choice), or, disillusioned by your breakup, they may have left the lives of both you and your ex. You may have decided to shed others, seeing that they could no longer contribute to your life in a positive way.

Losing people in the wake of a breakup can be yet another painful aspect of the experience, but you might be surprised to find that it can also be quite a relief. The space created by the exit of some people allows for new members of your community to shine and often lets old members play more important parts than they could in the past. Instead of a community based on the ups and downs of your romantic life, you now have the opportunity to choose exactly whom you wish to invest in, gaining the chance to build a wide, varied, and comfortable safety net that supports you while letting you be exactly who you are.

In some ways, you're likely very different from the person you were before your breakup. Of course, the fundamentals of your personality are still intact, but a painful breakup can change the way you feel about a number of important life issues. Just as your attitudes may have changed about how you see yourself and what you want, the role you play in your community may also have changed.

Couple Culture

It may seem strange at first that you're no longer seen by your friends and family as part of a couple. Maybe that means you're no longer getting invited to those dinner parties where everyone is coupled off. Or, perhaps you feel out of the loop when your friends are all talking about their sweeties. In this culture, where pairing up is so important, a couple can be useful in assuring other couples that they've made the right choice by being in a serious relationship.

Some friends, especially those who are coupled, may seem a bit put off by your new single status. They may not know exactly how to treat you and may not understand how you're feeling. And, unfortunately, many couples seem to take a friend's breakup as some sort of a bad omen, a signal that all is not right in the world of coupledom. Lynn found that her single status made her see the world in a somewhat compartmentalized way, especially when friends seemed to be avoiding her:

It did seem very segregated—either everybody is single and on the make, which is not where I wanted to be, or coupled and acting almost as if the breakup would be catching.

As a newly single woman, Lynn may have been somewhat threatening to her coupled friends. This may be because there still exists the notion that a single woman can be dangerous. This idea, archaic but deep-seated in our culture, holds that a single woman is unregulated and likely to do unruly things—like steal another person's mate. This may seem hopelessly dated to you, but it's possible that it's still lurking under the surface of your friendships.

Even if your friends seem pretty comfortable with your single status, some may still offer subtle cues that they'd like to see you paired up again. Caring friends might try to set you up with someone new right away in an effort to help you forget about your ex. They want to see you happy and with someone who deserves you. This may be a sign that they want you back in the coupled world—that they don't quite know how to relate to you as an individual. Or they may simply want to offer you a distraction. Either way, it can put you in an awkward situation when friends announce they've found the "perfect" person for you. You may warm to the idea, but most of the women we spoke with found that this assistance came a bit too quickly, before they were ready to even start contemplating someone new. Renee saw her coupled friends' matchmaking as a generous act—just ill-timed:

My couple friends didn't withdraw at all. They were very supportive. They did try to matchmake a little bit more than they should have, sooner than they should have. But I don't feel like I've lost any couple friends.

You have the right to tell your overly helpful friends that, though you appreciate their concern and might want to take them up on their offer later, you need more time to heal before dating. Usually, caring friends back right off, giving you all the space you need.

How Your Friends React

You may have been surprised at the various reactions you saw in your friends when they heard about your breakup. They may have been shocked, or they may have seen it coming from a long way off. Many women find that their friends, who are often privy to the troubles going on in the relationship, are glad it has finally come to an end. It can really open your eyes to discover that your friends are happy that you broke up. Barbara discovered the strain her friends had gone through in witnessing the strife in her relationship. Many of her friends welcomed the extra space in her life:

The breakup strengthened my one-on-one relationships with my friends. Before, they would come over and we were both around. Sometimes it was tense, because Maggie and I would fight a lot—it was a volatile relationship. A lot of times things would come up when our friends were there. And I was a different kind of person. I would say, "Table it until the guests leave." But she'd say, "No way! It's happening now, we deal with it now." So it was always like, "Excuse me, we're having a fight right now. Sorry if it's ruining your dinner." Later I realized that my friends thought it was really hard to be around us, and some of them were like, "It's so nice to see you without Maggie."

Other friends were just really shocked that we had broken up. They thought we were great together and that we would be together forever. But with my primary friends, it really strengthened our relationships. I had more time to spend with them and there wasn't that tension there that had been problematic.

If your relationship was rocky, your friends might have found witnessing it extremely painful. They may be sympathetic to the grief the breakup brought but also very relieved that you're out of a bad situation.

On the other hand, some of your friends may surprise you with a negative reaction. Even if they know all the problems that existed in your relationship, some friends may express dismay at the ending or be unwilling to acknowledge any pain you may be feeling. Some may be too uncomfortable with the suffering they see you going through to be able to help. They may urge you to forget it and move on right away. Anne found this attitude disconcerting and felt that her strong feelings were negated by her friend's flip response:

I remember telling a friend at work what had happened, and she snapped her finger and said, "Just give her up!" And I said, "Well, it's not that easy."

Acquaintances and even closer friends may be uncomfortable with the strong emotions you're experiencing. Perhaps they believe displays of emotion are better kept in private, or maybe they simply don't know how to respond in a helpful way. Other friends may have had certain ideas or expectations about your relationship that will no longer be met. They may feel let down by the breakup—as though you've squandered *their* dreams. Wendy left her boyfriend of five years after she realized she didn't want to make a lifetime commitment to him because he was too emotionally distant. She found that her friend was sad that they would not be traveling the same road together at the same time:

I think partly that Sandra is upset that we broke up, because that means that Peter and I aren't going to get married and have kids, like she did, and she wants me to do that so we can share it. So, I think she's sad 'cause her expectations weren't met.

Jeanette's friend was upset that her view of "the perfect relationship" wasn't true:

After we broke up, I was talking with an old friend, and it became obvious that she just loved our relationship. She totally romanticized it. And she was bummed that we had broken up. And it wasn't that she was upset for me—she was bummed for herself!

Friends who, consciously or unconsciously, expected you to live up to their dreams may not realize that their reactions are inappropriate to the situation. If you turn to friends for support and discover that their expectations for you prevent them from offering assistance, you can try looking to more accessible friends for the help you need. Or, if you feel up to it, you can let your unresponsive friends know what you need from them. When her boyfriend, Chad, ended their relationship and moved away, Zoë found herself faced with an unresponsive best friend:

I had to have a talk with my best friend, Cheryl. We'd been hanging out quite a bit after Chad left town, which provided a distraction. But, whenever I would start to talk about how I was feeling, she would get really uncomfortable and sort of laugh it off, which really hurt my feelings. So, eventually I just had to broach the subject with her. I said, "Cheryl, I get the feeling that hearing stuff about my breakup with Chad makes you sort of uncomfortable. Maybe you just don't know what to say, but I need to let you know that I'd like you to just listen, if you can. I really need that support from you now." And you know what?

*She actually started coming through. It was one of the hardest
conversations I've ever had with her, but it was worth it in the end.*

Family Responses

When you break the news to your family, they also may exhibit a
number of different emotions. You may have had an inkling about
your family's opinion of your ex, but even so, their reactions can surprise or disappoint you.

Your family may be very happy about the breakup because
they, like your friends, saw the problems you'd been dealing with in
the relationship. Or, they may be relieved that your relationship has
ended because they always had a problem with your ex. Julia's
grandma had always let her know that she would prefer that Julia
date a Jewish man, and when Julia's relationship ended, her reaction
came as no surprise:

*My grandmother was thrilled. When Jake and I first started going out
she asked, "Is he Jewish?" and I said, "No." And that was it for him.
She didn't even remember his name, I don't think. She used to call him
my "friend." It was like, "You mean the guy I'm living with and
sleeping in the same bed with?"*

If your family's reactions seem insensitive, it may help to
remember where they're coming from. If they hold traditional views
and if they suspected that your relationship might be a life partnership, of course they're relieved that you now have another chance to
make what they perceive to be the right choice.

If you were involved in a lesbian relationship you may find
your family's level of support depends on how they feel about your
sexual orientation. If your family is still in denial, they may be happy
that your relationship has ended and think that maybe now you'll
"grow out of it" or "change back." Even if your family is normally
supportive about other difficulties you face, they may have a blind
spot in regard to homosexuality and be unable to support you.

Your family may be sad about the breakup if there were expectations of permanence for the relationship. They may have wanted
you to get married, or at least give them some grandchildren, and
they may think you've just taken a big step back from those events.
They may also be saddened to lose your ex, with whom they've
grown close. Your parents may think of your ex as a son or daughter
and feel the loss keenly. Kids, who often don't feel shy about

expressing their feelings, can let you know that they really feel hurt when someone they'd bonded with is no longer in the picture. Nikki's niece and nephew not only felt they were losing an aunt and a godparent, but a second home as well:

My niece and nephew were affected greatly because, since the time they were born, we pretty much coparented them, even though they lived two hours away. They would come and spend weeks at a time at our house. They had their own drawers, their own closet full of toys. They grew up there. And so it's been really hard for them.

My niece, who is eight, brought it up to me. She said, "I understand. Sometimes grown-ups need space. Is it going to be very long?" My nephew, on the other hand—he's almost seven. He asked me about it and I told him we just needed some space for a while, and he said, "But it's been a while already, and I don't like this." He's not happy about it. To them it's always "Auntie Nikki and Auntie Marin." There's no separation. And now they've lost this environment that was theirs, too.

Children who feel that they're at risk of losing a parental figure or the home they cherish are naturally going to be hurt and frightened.

Other kids are hurt not by losing a parent or home, but by losing a cherished role model. Lucy's sisters had looked to her relationship to affirm their dream of romance and commitment, and found it painful when their expectations weren't met:

Talking to my little sisters about it was really hard. When I broke up with Robert, they were devastated. Robert was so close to them, he taught one of them how to ride her bike and one of them how to swim. He was really close with my family, and my sisters still talk about him. It's six years later, and they'll still ask, "Why did you break up with Robert, again?" And I had to try to explain these really complicated things in simple terms. I feel bad, because they've been through so many divorces, and they're like, "C'mon. Someone just get married and have a nice life and show us that people stay together."

The sad fact is that sometimes people don't stay together, and though it may hurt you not to fulfill the expectations of the kids in your life, it's impossible to protect them entirely from the realities of relationships. What you can do is reassure them about your love for them, which doesn't have to be affected by the success or failure of any other relationship in your life.

When Shannon's relationship ended, her brother reacted with pain and anger:

When we broke up, my brother was just devastated. And I'd even thought about that, too. I was like, "Oh, my God. If I leave this engagement my brother is going to be really disappointed." It's amazing how that delayed me, even when I knew it was time to break up. And my brother was really angry at me for a while. But also, he can look at it as an example: You've got to trust your heart. But, inevitably, you're going to disappoint people.

Your Family, Not Mine

You may have bonded quite closely to your ex's family, looking at them as family of your own. But, in the wake of your breakup, some family members may feel that loyalty to your ex means that they can no longer be close to you. This can really hurt—feeling like you're losing a mother, father, or sibling. And though this separation is not often met with resentment or bitterness, it can still cut you to the quick. Julia, who'd lost her mother to cancer a short time before her breakup, felt as though she was losing a mother all over again:

I loved the family. I bonded with his mom, probably because I didn't have one. But that was really hard. I remember calling her up and saying, "Well, Jake and I are breaking up." She and I had talked about our problems in the past so I don't think she was surprised. But when I actually broke up with him, I thought, "Oh, my God. I don't get to talk to his mom anymore." I sent her holiday cards and stuff like that, but she was very loyal. She would talk to me occasionally, but I knew that she was basically thinking, "Stay away. You ruined my son."

You may discover that your ex's parents are angry with you, feeling protective of their child. This can get right in the way of your relationship with them, sometimes making any continued contact impossible. Even if you don't experience any rancor from your ex's family, their feelings of loyalty may still mean that you lose them. Barbara felt that she got something from her ex's family that she never had with her family. Losing them felt in a way like losing a part of herself:

The thing that was the hardest for me was losing her family. They had been sort of my adopted American family. That's what I would call them, because they were very different from my family. You know, they were American, and I come from an immigrant family. So they would celebrate everything the "American" way. Like Thanksgiving, which my family rarely celebrated, and the Fourth of July. We would always go to her house and her father would be at the grill. And, it had taken a while, but I felt like her family had accepted me. It was really nice to be there—they were very generous. They were part of my family—in-laws, I suppose. I would spend holidays with them and we would vacation in the summer together. So it was really hard losing that family.

I actually got a letter from her mom a month ago. Her mom used to clip things out of the paper and send them to us. That's another thing I felt I lost—that connection. But I got this letter a month ago with this little note saying, "We still think of you, and we thought you would be interested in this clipping from the paper." It was really very sweet.

Even if you, like Barbara, are able to maintain some contact with your ex's family, the relationship is almost invariably altered for the worse after the breakup. This can compound the feelings of loss you experience from the breakup itself.

Clare was worried when she broke up that she would lose her close relationship with her ex's mother. Luckily, she found that, because the basis of their relationship had been a mutual admiration rather than discussion of her boyfriend, they could still be close:

I still talk to his mom. We don't talk about him—we never have. But now she refers to me as "My young friend, Clare," instead of "my son's girlfriend." She met me through her son, but we have a relationship apart from that.

On the other hand, you may feel a strong sense of relief at the prospect of cutting ties to your ex's family. Perhaps you never really got along with them or felt they judged you. The fact that you no longer have to expend any energy dealing with them can feel quite liberating. Hannah was fond of her ex's family, but felt that her investment in them had become a burden:

I like his family, and I think that they're really good people, but I'm really happy not to have to make that schlep to his hometown and sit around their house, talking to his mom. It was such a duty, a chore. And it was always my chore—he would let me do all the talking. So I had to do his family work for him, and I really resented it.

But, even if losing your ex's family feels like a relief, it's almost always tinged with a bit of pain, as it symbolizes the end of your romantic relationship. If you find it painful to lose your former partner's family, you can take some comfort in the knowledge that the loss likely has nothing to do with *you*. You're not necessarily being rejected personally by people you love. Instead, it's really just a sad matter of circumstance.

Whose Friends Are Whose?

While it's usually fairly clear who "gets" which family member, splitting up friends can be more difficult. Sometimes you haven't particularly bonded with your ex's friends and vice versa. But, if you have a group of friends who are intimate with both of you, you may find yourself wondering who will go and who will stay. In *Uncoupling*, Diane Vaughan explains that the competition for who gets which friend can be fierce, as important ties are severed and you feel the loss of your breakup compounded by the loss of good friends.

This competition over friends may be overt, or you may hardly see it, often depending on how messy your breakup has been. After the breakup of their fourteen-month relationship seven years ago, Elizabeth's ex tried to make it very clear which friends she considered her property:

There was a lot of confusion about friends, since I had become very fond of some of her friends, and I was "forbidden" to talk to them. Some I let go, others I kept in contact with for varying lengths of time.

You may have to decide if you want to fight to keep certain people in your life, or you can try negotiating with your former partner about it. Sitting down and talking to your ex about how you're going to deal with mutual friends, or talking to your friends about their role in your postbreakup life, may seem awkward or even ridiculous. But, in a difficult situation, sometimes seemingly ridiculous actions are the only options available.

You may be faced with an ex who is so angry that he or she makes a conscious effort to claim mutual friends. But even if the breakup is amicable, friends of a couple often feel forced to choose sides. Authors D. Merilee Clunis and G. Dorsey Green offer suggestions for ways to avoid some of this division: The couple can sit their friends down and talk to them together about the breakup and how they would like their friends to treat each partner. Or the exes can make an effort to speak respectfully about their former partner in front of friends and ask friends to avoid taking sides. The authors are careful to point out, however, that sometimes, despite these efforts, you can't avoid losing certain friends.

It may be a Herculean task to try and split friends amiably because raw emotions and inevitably stretched loyalties complicate the matter. Renee tried to manage the separation of friends with her ex, with mixed results:

The night that we broke up, my partner said, "You'll get all of the friends. They're all yours anyway." And I said, "It doesn't have to be that way. We don't have to go for each other's throats, we don't have to tear each other apart. They're your friends, too." And I was such a fucking saint, I can't believe it. I actually called several friends and said, "Look. Bree thinks everyone is going to turn on her and hate her, and you've gotta know that there's a part of me that's hugely relieved by this breakup, so she's not wholly the bad guy here. Please make an extra effort to let her know you're still there for her." And one friend said to me about six months later, "Do I still have to be friends with her? I really didn't like her."

Many times you can actually manage to share friends, but only if the rules are clear. Maria and her ex split some friends and shared others:

Some friends ended up making a choice, and pretty much couldn't stand her—had a really hard time with what she did. So, she lost some relationships. One couple we both stay in touch with, but they don't talk to me about her, and vice versa—that's the rule.

Whether it's a formal agreement or not, declining to talk trash about someone else's friend is a pretty basic level of respect. Denise and her ex had the extra consideration of their children and the relationship the children had to family friends.

Our friends have been very understanding. And they've taken the position of not being judgmental of either of us. I think part of that might be because we have children, so our closest friends are also extended family for our children. I'm very grateful for their loyalty to the kids.

In other instances friends may not come through for you, even when you let them know how they can help. While letting go of friends who do not come through for you can be hard, part of this renovation process is deciding who actually makes positive contributions in your life, and discarding those people who drag you down. Maria felt let down by two friends in her moment of great need and decided not to have those people remain in her life:

I remember going to some friends' houses for dinner a few days after Terri had told me it was over, and these friends had to see the sequel to some movie instead of talking with me. And I just said, "Forget it." I mean, I was suicidal, in the depths of depression, and they had to see a movie? That was it.

We each have the power and the absolute right to decide who should and who should not be in our lives. If someone is not supportive of you or not healthy to have around, it may be time to tell them to hit the highway.

Runnin' with a New Crowd

Losing people from your former community may have left you with an unpleasant sense of the ephemeral nature of human relationships. People do come and go in our lives—that's the way of the world. But, as melancholy as this loss can make us feel, it also leaves space for new relationships to move in and fill the void left over from the past. The flexibility and changeability of relationships means that we're always free to add new people to our lives, people who'll love and accept us for who we are.

Some of the women we spoke to began to renovate their community even before they broke up. A lot of them felt that their new friends helped them leave their unfulfilling romantic relationship. Hannah found herself moving away from friendships she shared with her ex that she found unsatisfying, while at the same time meeting interesting people at a new job. This influx of new energy and support helped her feel safe enough to leave her unhappy relationship:

I think that a big reason that I could break up with Scott was that I'd made a bunch of new friends. And I can't even say how happy I am that I now have all of these people in my life. I didn't get along with Scott's friends—they were a burden to me. Trying to deal with them was like knocking my head against the wall. And now I have all of these new friends who I actually do enjoy, who like me—it just makes a world of difference. I feel like I wasted a lot of time trying to make friends with people I didn't choose—people I didn't like and who didn't like me. My new friendships and old friendships that have gotten stronger have been some of the best things about the breakup. I've discovered that my friends are my safety net, but it's not the same as leaning on a big crutch, like I did in my relationship.

New people in your life can help you see the possibilities before you—what your life *could* be. This new vision can help you leave a relationship, or encourage you to spread your wings after you've left. Hannah's first big outing after her breakup opened her eyes to the joyous possibilities that awaited her:

I moved out at the end of June, and Fourth of July was the next weekend after that. I went out with my friend Kate and a bunch of her friends who I didn't know very well. We went out and saw fireworks, drank whiskey, and had a lot of fun. Then we went back to Kate's house and stayed up until three singing, and I spent the night. It was really nice. I didn't have to check in with anyone, I could stay out as long as I wanted, no one was home worrying about me, no one would be jealous. I could go out and have a really good time for a silly reason—Fourth of July, who cares—but we could just go out and celebrate and have a good time. And I was meeting all these people I liked, who liked me. And I felt really good. I thought, "Wow, this is what my life could be like."

The new freedom in your life may at times be scary, but if you try to look at it as an opportunity and embrace the wonderful feeling of newness it can give, you can experience a unique sense of exhilaration.

You may find that you're not only open to new sorts of people, but also to new ways of meeting people. Maria, a lawyer, decided to take advantage of a number of professional groups to meet new people:

I made a big effort to be more social pretty early on. I went to a bunch of group things—professional women's events. So I met a lot of people whom I like and would never have met otherwise. And that helped.

You usually have to exert some effort to mingle with new people after your breakup, but you don't always have to do it face to face. Rachel discovered the ease and comfort of online relationships:

I have this online community, so that when I'm home I can get online and read mail from friends and e-mail them whenever I need to. It has sort of been a daily infusion of connection. One of my e-mail friends called me the other day, actually. This woman from New Jersey gave me a call on Valentine's Day and said, "How are you doing? I know this is a hard day for people just breaking up." I mean, she's not my best friend, she's just a concerned person who I get along with online. And another woman I'd met online mailed me chocolate! Those little touches can really help.

It can be tremendously exciting to feel your social world opening up to new possibilities and people, though it's not always automatic. The vacuum that your breakup left will begin to fill with new people if you're open to them and go after them. If you feel short on new friendships, try some of the things the women we interviewed tried: go to professional groups, go online, take classes, get involved in a political cause, or volunteer in your community. Follow your interests and seek out what makes you happy, and new people will naturally be attracted to you.

This period of change in your life may make you open to a whole lot of new people and things, but you may also be feeling a little burned. You may find that, though you're open in some ways, you're also more discriminating about who you want in your life. Lynn now feels that she wants friends who match her changed values:

I'm a lot pickier about my friends. Before, if my friends had sort of fuzzy sexual boundaries with other people, it was like, "Well, all right, whatever, we're still friends." But because one of my friends slept with my partner, without a second thought, my feelings about that have changed.

Because it's now entirely your choice who you want to associate with, you're free to set any conditions to friendship you wish. When you're burned badly by an unhappy relationship, the repercussions may spread to many parts of your life.

Along with new friendships that are opening to you, your old friendships may have moved into positions of greater prominence in the wake of your breakup. You've likely needed a lot of support, and hopefully your old friends have been able to step in and offer it. There's more room in your life for friendships now that your romantic relationship isn't taking up your time and energy, and your old friends may really appreciate seeing more of you. Barbara found that reaching out to old friends provided necessary help and a welcome invitation to intimacy:

One of the things I was aware of when she first moved out was just how alone I was. So, I was always on the phone to my friends. I would just go down the list thinking, "Who haven't I called?" I saw a lot more of my friends than I did before. I had them come over and hang out with me, stay over.

Many women find that they've lost touch with old friends while wrapped up in their romantic endeavors. If you'd like to reconnect and need the support your friends can bring, don't be afraid to reach out and ask for help. Most likely, your friends will be glad for the opportunity to get close to you again.

Over and over the women we interviewed told us how new friendships and the deepening of old friendships was one of the very best things about breaking up. The space and energy they'd previously used for their romantic relationships could now be used to enrich their communities, building strong and various groups that helped them thrive.

With a Little Help from My Friends

You're probably well aware of how important the support of your community can be. Most women run smack into the need for a wider community when they go through a breakup and no longer have that one person they'd counted on to help. Then, they naturally move closer to the people they do have.

It's wonderful to feel our friends and family lending their help to get us through hard times. And this sort of support is one reason we want to continue having these people in our lives. Some of your most harrowing or painful moments have been lightened by the people you choose to have in your circle of support. Renee talked about the loving care she received early on:

They rallied around as if there had been a death. Casseroles came in, and people did sort of a death watch on the following weekend. It was like, "Jesus! Can't I get any time alone?" But I knew that it was just their love and concern—they knew how devastated I was.

The profound pain you experience after your breakup can be surprising in its intensity. It's important to have people around you who understand and try to lighten your load. These are the people you know will be there when you call. It took Denise a long while to start feeling better, and she had to repeatedly ask for help from her friends:

It took me months to adjust. I'd put a movie on for the kids and bring my phone into the bathroom. I'd call one of my best friends and I'd just sit and cry and say, "I don't know if I can do this."

When she felt desperate, Denise could reach out and get the help she needed. Sometimes you need to ask for support instead of waiting around for people to offer. Your friends may not always know when you need them.

You may be surprised at the support you find and where you find it. Often, even people you wouldn't expect to find help from recognize a person in need and come through in heartfelt and gratifying ways. Nikki felt very cared for in her professional realm, a place that had never been personal before:

I don't talk about my personal business at work much, but I found that I was so into just taking care of me that I became very relaxed about it. And people in my office were so supportive. Even the men. There are a couple of them who are friends of mine, but a couple of them are sort of macho. And they've just been really, really sweet. And that's been nice for me—I've been able to sort of come out, in a way, and not be judged at all.

The cataclysmic changes a breakup brings can have repercussions throughout your life, often breaking down barriers between you and other people—people you never thought would come through for you.

If you're close to your family, they can also be a source of powerful support. You may be surprised to find that, even if your family hadn't acknowledged the seriousness of your relationship in the past, they're willing to respond to your pain and lend a hand. Lucy was able to bond particularly with her dad, who helped her when she woke up in a panic:

My parents were supportive of the intensity of the feelings overall. Even though we weren't married, we were in the same age group as they were when they got married. I felt like they understood. I would call my dad at six o'clock in the morning—you know those breakup mornings where you just wake up—"Bing!" And I would call my dad and he would say, "I understand. It's awful."

Your needs may have the effect of drawing family members closer to you, reaffirming the bonds you feel for each other. Many women with children find that their kids can be a wonderfully loving source of support. Anne's fourteen-year-old son always helped lift her flagging spirits:

My son has been really good. He says, "Mom, you're really cute, you're young. Go out there, have fun—it's okay. She bogged you down." So, he's been really good. He's a great guy.

It can be wonderful to feel the support and unconditional love a child can offer, but you also need to be careful not to lean too heavily on your kids. They look to you for strength and are also affected by the breakup.

Though your community is where you turn for support, sometimes the people who populate it don't exactly know how to offer support, or are afraid to reach out. Nikki sometimes found support lacking because too many people were afraid of seeming to take sides in her breakup, so they just stayed away:

It's almost like people are afraid they're going to get in the middle, so they just stay on the sidelines. And it's been kind of hurtful in that you think, "You know, they could just call and say, 'How are you?'"

You may be hurt by seemingly neglectful friends, or you may wish some friends had left well enough alone. Even the best-meaning friends can botch their attempts at helping you, sometimes making you feel even worse. In their attempts to cheer her up with platitudes, Maria's friends only served to alienate her:

Other friends told me that a year from then I would feel much better. And all of that I considered to be offensive. Don't tell me it's going to be better. I know they were all trying to do their best, but it was like, at that time there was no better.

This is a case of "too little, too early," with friends trying to get Maria's chin up instead of supporting her in her grief. Sometimes you may need to ask your friends to just let you feel the way you're feeling and not try to cheer you up.

Another common way friends can botch their attempts to help is to take your anger on as theirs, railing against your ex in a way that effectively usurps your role. Barbara had one friend who only seemed interested in talking, not listening:

I was friends with this woman who had broken up with her girlfriend a year earlier. Sometimes I liked talking to her about it. But she'd had this nasty breakup and she was into being nasty about it. She would say about my girlfriend, "Oh, she's a jerk," or whatever. And I felt like she wasn't totally a jerk. I felt like I couldn't even vent about it because she was venting for me.

A breakup can kick up all kinds of emotions in other people, and sometimes these emotions may come spilling out. If this happens, you can either stay away from those who have a tendency to spew at you, or you can take the initiative to explain to them exactly what you need and what you don't want. A few words of clarification can set them back on the track to helping you.

They Say It Takes a Village

As you set about redesigning and renovating your life after your breakups, you'll probably give some thought to the makeup of the community you would now like to have around you. You've probably lost some people and gained some others over the course of your postbreakup process, and the question of what kind of community you'd like to build around yourself may weigh on your mind.

After her breakup, Maria made a conscious effort to cast her social net a bit wider:

I was, for me, extremely social afterwards. I was really thinking I never again wanted to put all of my eggs in just one basket. I had this incredible need to develop a life that was not dependent upon one person, who could, through her actions, devastate me. So I started a lot of new relationships.

Maria was determined not to slide back into her old habits of dependence on just one other person, so she made every effort to build a strong network of support, a community that not only supports her as part of a group, but as an individual as well.

Many of the women we spoke to had realized the importance of developing this network and had worked hard to create a wider social circle. As their romantic relationships receded, they found themselves looking at their platonic relationships differently. Many found that friendships had taken center stage once their primary romantic relationship had self-destructed. Clare saw her friends in a new light after her breakup:

The day after we broke up, I was going around to my friends, talking about it. They were all trying to help, and that's the first glimpse I got of my friendships—my female friends—and how important they were. And I just felt so good. I thought, "Yeah! This is so cool!" I was totally happy. And it wasn't because of him—it was because of my friends and me.

Many women find that the lack of effort they put into their friendships during their relationship comes back to haunt them. Sarah said:

I felt really guilty, actually, when I got out of my relationship because I felt like I was suddenly asking for support from people who I didn't always have around me during the relationship. So, in the beginning it was kind of hard to ask for help. But I found that everyone responded in one way or another, in the early stages of my recovery.

Asking for help can be hard, even if you stayed close to your friends during your relationship. But, if you're going to get what you need, you may have to come right out and ask for it. Being clear about your needs is always the best way to get them met. Most of the women we spoke with found that even distant friends came to their aid.

Many women resolve to maintain stronger bonds with friends, whether they're single or are involved with a romantic partner. Hannah talked about how crucial it is to maintain those connections:

My dependence on friends after my breakup really emphasized something I've always believed but haven't always lived up to, which is that even if you're perfectly happy with your romantic partner, you have to work hard and put effort into keeping your friends around. Because you shouldn't always be hanging out with or depending on one person too much—it's not healthy.

You may also come to realize that your emotional health is better served by you and a whole group of loving friends than by you and one other person alone. But what happens if you fall in love again? Many of the women we spoke to said that even if they do begin a new romantic relationship, their priorities would be more wide-ranging than they were before. As Jeanette put it:

I'd always been really close to my female friends, and valued them, but I hadn't understood how important that network was. When Chris and I broke up, I hadn't talked to my oldest friend in a year. I mean, we had totally separate lives, and we didn't have any idea what the other was doing. I know now that in future romantic relationships, my partner will be a priority, but not the priority.

Part III

Settling In

Chapter 6

Putting Your Ex
into Storage

I'm really glad Peter and I have managed to stay close. I have to say, it hasn't been easy—we had to work out a lot of stuff before we found a place that was comfortable for both of us. But, we just know each other so well, and I think we each value and love so many things about each other. I'm so happy I haven't had to give up knowing him.

—Wendy

The last time we had a friendly, sociable time together, she told me over brunch that her new partner was having a really bad time with menopause and wasn't responding well to the drugs, and actually liked gin an awful lot, and was something of an abusive drunk, and that they were moving to New Orleans in August. I sat there and I swear, I didn't crack a smile, I didn't. But I thought, "You're moving to the murder capital of the United States, in the hottest month, with a woman who's an abusive drunk having a really bad menopause—thank you, Jesus!"

—Renee

I have to keep in mind that closure is not going to be how I want things to end. It's an acceptance of what happened and what I went through.

—Nikki

While the progression isn't exactly neat and tidy, once we've survived ground zero and worked our way through most of the rebuilding of our selves and our communities we'll be ready to begin settling into our new lives. This is when we can start reaping the benefits of all of our hard work, all of the grieving and reassessment and restructuring.

It's time to get a move on—with your life, that is. Suddenly you find that, if you've really processed and accepted the past, you're raring to jump headlong into your new life—with a vigor and enthusiasm you never could have imagined when you were in the throes of ground zero or in the midst of reconstruction. This is the time to really assess your possibilities and focus your attention on the present and the future. There'll likely be some stumbling blocks, but all in all it'll be full speed ahead.

Can We Still Be Friends?

The phrase "Let's be friends" is the über-cliché of breakups. Why do so many people cringe when they hear it? Maybe it's because too many people, trying to let their lover down gently, say they want to be friends when they don't really mean it. Or perhaps it's because it sounds like a consolation prize ("I don't want to share my life with you anymore. But, hey, don't worry. We can still hang out once and a while!"). The cynics in a crowd will tell you that they hate the hackneyed breakup promise because it never really comes true, because it's impossible to truly make the transition from lover to friend.

But what if you really *do* want to be friends? What if you meant what you said, even if it was something that's been said a thousand times before? What does it feel like to actually stay friends with your ex? Well, it ain't easy, but a few of the women we talked to were able to remain close friends with their ex-partners. Wendy, who ended her relationship with Peter when she decided she didn't want to get married, has found that having Peter as a friend has enriched her life:

I'm really glad Peter and I have managed to stay close. I have to say, it hasn't been easy—we had to work out a lot of stuff before we found a place that was comfortable for both of us. But, we just know each other so well, and I think we each value and love so many things about each other. I'm so happy I haven't had to give up knowing him.

The criteria that seemed most common in terms of who remained friends was how respectful the breakup was. Not that there hadn't been any arguments or angry words, but that, in general, the breakup occurred without lies, infidelities, or actions that felt like betrayals. As Wendy put it, "I'm *not* friends with the man I dated before Peter, because he totally screwed me over and cheated on me. When the whole thing was over I felt nothing but contempt for him."

Even if there hasn't been a betrayal, the work of rebuilding a friendship with an ex is complicated. While Hannah and her ex are still close, she'll be the first to admit that establishing new roles in their relationship hasn't been easy:

The boundaries are sort of weird. He still wants me to be his big supporter—his emotional girlfriend. And he still needs me to help him with all of his emotional work, complaining to me and asking for advice. Sometimes I resent it. Then, on top of that, he wants to talk to me about dating, and I don't really want to talk to him about that.

As you struggle to move forward and get on with your life, it can get tricky carving out a new niche for your ex, especially if he or she is having trouble shifting gears in the relationship.

Even if you work hard with a former partner who is flexible, you can encounter emotional stumbling blocks left over from the past. For example, old feelings about formerly important days and dates can swoop down to cloud your new friendship. When you know someone intimately, whether or not he or she remains a part of your daily life, that person's routines and lifestyles are impressed into your consciousness. And when these significant dates hit, you may have no way to deal with your old emotions and feelings of loss in the structure of the new relationship with your ex. As Hannah found, these emotional echoes can make maintaining a friendship harder:

It's still sometimes difficult staying friends with him. The thing is that I really love Scott, and I think he's a great person. He's really funny and smart, and I would love to be friends with him, even if we hadn't dated. But because we have dated and broken up, there is this whole separation of our worlds now, and the more that time passes the more it feels like we're drifting apart.

His birthday was two weeks ago, and it was still so strange not to be planning something for him. We got together for a beer a few days after his actual birthday, and I gave him some small gifts—nothing as fancy as I would have given him before. The whole experience really made me feel how much space was between us. It made me kind of sad to see those small presents sitting there on the table.

Whether your ex is celebrating with friends or a new lover, or going through a personal crisis or transition of some sort, you're likely to experience uncertainty or regret regarding your new role as friend. You may also be left with the difficult task of negotiating a new relationship and unlearning past automatic behaviors that are no longer appropriate with your ex.

But, as tough as reworking your romantic relationship into a friendship can be, it's not impossible. Time and growth can help your friendship with your ex bloom, even if the beginning seems rocky. You may find that baggage and communication problems recede after time—after both of you have moved forward and left much of the relationship in the past. Friendship can be made smoother after both of you have gone on to date other people and feel secure in the growth you've made away from the romantic relationship. Even if you don't expect it, you may find yourself befriending your ex further on down the road, when it feels safer.

Many women decide that trying to stay completely away from their ex-partners is their best option, giving them the space they need to heal without the reminder of seeing an ex. For some, seeing an ex feels like the opening of a wound that's trying to heal. Anne couldn't handle contact with her ex, even though her former girlfriend was still very much dependent on her:

We used to call each other during the day. After we split, I would go to the phone, dial her number—and hang up. Because I couldn't call her anymore. We weren't partners. We weren't lovers. And that's what hits me hardest. Something comes up in my life and I want to call her up and talk to her about it. And I can't.

She wants to be friends, and I can't make that switch. I can't be her friend when I was the partner in her life. She calls every day. I think she looks for reasons to call. And I have to tell her, "Don't call me. You don't need to call me." But she keeps calling.

Many women feel that if they continue to see their former partners after the breakup, they may slide back into wanting to renew the relationship. Whether you were the leaver or the leavee in the breakup, you may choose to keep your distance if the pull of nostalgia and the power of your old dreams still draws you back. Sabine found her old partner's romantic gestures to her very unsettling:

I saw him a year after we broke up. He actually got back together with the woman he dated before me. And it was fine. But I was talking to him, reconnecting, or whatever, and he just started getting all mushy on me. And I thought, "I'm just saying 'hi,' okay? You're living with your girlfriend now. Don't trip me out."

When you've closed a door and someone opens it again, you're not sure if you want to see what's in there. I mean, I don't want to go backwards in my life.

Continuing a relationship keeps some women from moving on with their lives. As Joan puts it, "I'm glad that I was smart enough to know that I had to make a clean break with Carl in order to lead my own separate life." A sense of independence and progress is important for many women.

Some of us can't see our ex-lovers because we're afraid we'll slide backward in a very specific way: by getting sexually reinvolved. Rachel found her contact with her ex emotionally turbulent because they would end up in each other's arms, rekindling old fires and opening old wounds:

I've had to really cut her off. I tend to have issues with boundaries, and if I'm seeing her, I'd be afraid I would start saying, "Why did we have to break up?" And start begging her. I know that's really bad for me. The other thing is, the last time we saw each other we ended up having sex. I know that a lot of couples do that kind of stuff, but it really put me on an emotional roller coaster.

Though falling into bed with an ex can feel comforting in the moment, many women feel depleted, sad, and confused afterward when they realize that the relationship is still over.

On the other hand, if you want to have sex with your former partner and you feel that it won't confuse you emotionally, there's nothing intrinsically "wrong" about that decision. Lily, who continued to live with her ex-boyfriend for a few weeks after the breakup, saw it as a way to meet her needs:

I just really wanted to be intimate with him before it was completely over. I suggested it, and he asked if it would mean we were getting back together. I was very clear that it had nothing to do with that. And I don't regret those times with him. It was more about getting my physical needs met and also saying good-bye to our relationship. I didn't find it confusing at all. For me, breakup sex was great sex.

The general consensus with the women we talked to was that you need to be clear with yourself and your partner about what it is you're looking for from your interactions.

Most of the women who were betrayed by their ex felt no desire to attempt a friendship because the foundation of trust necessary to friendship was gone. Lily feels that her ex-partner's lies made him ineligible for her friendship:

I always thought we would be best friends. If I had ever thought we could break up, I was sure we would always be friends. And maybe if he had said, "Well, you know what? I'm feeling like you don't really want to be with me and I just can't deal with it, so we need to break up," I think we would still be friends today. But because he had to be so circuitous about it and because he lied to me, we couldn't be friends.

Some women are very firm in their desires not to see or hear from their former partners, while others prefer to leave their options open. Nikki, who ended her relationship nine months earlier and currently has no contact with her ex, wants to wait and see:

Right now I'm staying away from her until I'm stronger. I kind of see it as being like a junkie or an alcoholic. When you first decide that you're going to stop drinking, you don't hang out in bars, you don't hang out with friends who say, "Here, have a drink." So I'm just staying away until I feel strong enough, because I feel like emotions go through a natural process of healing. Staying away is giving me a chance to heal. And when I get stronger, I'll reconnect with her, and the closure will naturally come.

Thirty-one-year-old Daphne's partner had broken up their six-month relationship because she was uncomfortable with the level of commitment Daphne wanted from her. After the split nine months ago, Daphne found that she wasn't able to choose whether she wanted to maintain contact, because her ex didn't wish to have contact with her. This lack of control in the matter can feel frustrating, rejecting, and hurtful:

She put down that barrier: "I won't see you. I need to get over this by myself." I was made to feel as if I was this terrible clinging child, just weighing on her neck. It was just a horrible, humiliating picture.

If this is your situation, it's important to keep in mind that you don't necessarily need to have contact with your ex in order to make your own peace with the relationship and move on with your life. Plenty of the women we spoke to found resolution without the help of their ex.

Unfortunately, "help" is not how some of us would characterize what we get from our former partners. Yet, many women who would prefer to keep their distance from their exes are forced to stay in contact for practical reasons. You may have to see each other to transfer the kids on weekends, or to visit the pets. Perhaps you're in the middle of trying to sell the house you owned with your ex and are having to talk the details out. Whatever the reason, being forced to maintain contact can make for a difficult situation, with emotions from the breakup inevitably getting caught in the mix. Nikki finally had to put her foot down, dividing up responsibilities and asking for no contact:

We would go through stages where we would say, "Okay, we're not going to have contact. We really need space." But then she would call and say, "The pool's caving in, could you go to the house and take care of it?" Or, "I got this thing in the mail. What does it mean?" And so there was always something that came up where we would have to have contact. So now I'm just drawing the line and saying, "That's it. I'm not taking care of any more bills. Here's yours. Here's mine. Deal with it."

Matters can become extremely confusing when kids are involved. Denise, who adopted a child with her partner, knew she would have to continue to have her ex in her life because of their son:

Sometimes I wish my partner had died. Because the minute I realized it was definitely a reality and she was leaving, I also realized that I was stuck with her in my life—like it or not—because we had a four-year-old together.

It's at the point now where I've asked to have only one, maximum two, e-mails a week, and phone calls only if it's an emergency. For the longest time, I just couldn't hear her voice. I can't have her voice in my life.

If you're forced to have contact because of business or practical matters, you can still determine the rules of the game. How much contact is okay with you and in what form? You can decide what your boundaries will be in the situation and strictly enforce them. This will allow you to operate on a fairly civilized and emotionally smooth basis with your former partner and will let him or her know what you consider appropriate behavior.

You may find that your ex-lover's boundaries prevent you from dealing with the emotional baggage you wanted him or her to help you unpack. If your ex-partner doesn't want to have contact, or if he or she refuses to talk with you about the past, you may have to work out these issues on your own. Daphne wanted to deal with old issues in any friendship she'd have with her ex, and without that opportunity, a friendship wasn't worthwhile for her:

We did meet once a few months later, and I said, "Do you think at some point in the future we could talk about the past?" And she looked at me, and hesitated for a long time, then said, "No." So I just thought, well, if we can't talk about the past, what's the point?

This conflict of needs could be a matter of timing—one person being "over" the relationship before the other—but if one of you wants to process what has happened and the other doesn't, you might have to decide to leave friendship for a later time.

Basic components of a good friendship are trust and honesty. As we discussed earlier in the chapter, lies told during your past romantic relationship can make the trust necessary for a friendship impossible. While many women refuse contact with their exes in this situation, Lynn was willing to try and make it work. But when she broached the subject of trust with her ex, she realized that Brit didn't really want to invest in the friendship:

I said, "Neither one of us trusts the other one. How do you suggest that we begin to build trust if we're going to have a friendship?" And her response to me was, "You mean we're not friends?" And it was like, "No, of course we're not friends." At that moment I realized that she wasn't going to try to work it out.

If you have trouble trusting your ex and he or she seems unwilling to discuss the events that facilitated this distrust, it may be best to put hopes of a friendship on the shelf.

Hannah's friends, who saw all the problems she had with her ex in their romantic relationship, wondered why she chose to stay friends with him:

No one thought it would work, us being friends. His friends and mine were so surprised. But I felt like, "Of course we'll be friends. We really love each other." I guess it just depends on how hard we want to work at it.

You may feel a lot of pressure from others in your social circle either to stay friends or to break contact, but ultimately you need to let your emotions guide you, not the opinions of others.

You may also have friends who expect you to remain friends with your ex as a matter of course. Author Judith McDaniel found that many lesbians feel particular pressure to stay friends with their former partners because of the myth that lesbians "always" stay friends. But, McDaniel asks, why should lesbians who go through a gut-wrenching breakup get less acknowledgment than the women who are able to maintain friendships with their exes?

Elizabeth put all of those expectations aside and chose to remain separate from her ex:

Don't automatically give in to the assumption in some lesbian communities that the goal is to be friends with your ex. If you want to, fine. In my case, I felt terribly betrayed. Why would I want to be friends with someone who betrayed me?

If you're trying to decide whether or not to remain friends, D. Merilee Clunis and G. Dorsey Green offer some questions you may want to ask yourself:

> [W]hat kind of relationship do you want to have with each other after the breakup? What kind of commitment is each of you willing to make toward that goal? If you both agree that you want to be friends, you need to negotiate the terms of your friendship. What are your wants and expectations? How much time are you willing to spend to work out this transition from lovers to friends? Do you need to consider having a third party—a counselor, for example—help in this process? Does either one of you need time apart, without contact at all? (240)

Essentially, whether you remain friends depends on what you can offer each other in this new form of your relationship. Some women find that, after the romance has died, there isn't much left to hold them to their partner:

Zoë, who had tried to stay friends with her ex after he moved out of state, discovered that, when all was said and done, she didn't have much in common with him:

We call each other every once in a while. But, after he moved, it wasn't very long before I realized that we no longer had much to say to each other. I mean, we had the past to talk about. But with no promise of a future together, the dynamic was totally different. It was like, "Why should I care what's happening to you when it has absolutely nothing to do with my life?"

Clare's feelings as her perception of her ex changed were more decisive:

The last time I saw him, I just thought "Pig!" The time before that I had thought he was so sweet still. But this time I could only think what a coward he was, how weak he was.

Postbreakup feelings and fast-changing lifestyles can exacerbate the differences that caused you and your ex to break up, or they can make you see a whole "new" side of him or her. Like Zoë, you may question your own perceptions. Of course, it's common to see your lover through rose-colored glasses during the relationship. Strange habits are seen as sweet quirkiness. But when the relationship ends, you may suddenly see your ex in a different way. And, over time, this may change your feelings about maintaining a friendship.

For many of us, time is not the issue. Lots of us decide almost right away to exclude our exes from our new lives. Some make this decision in order to minimize the ongoing impact that goes along with seeing their ex-partners' changing lives. Others make it for reasons of personal safety, mental well-being, or simple personal preference. Whatever the reason, this decision has both advantages and disadvantages. The major disadvantage is that someone who was once integral in your life is now completely out of the picture. Jeanette talked about her feelings regarding her choice not to continue having contact with her ex, and how they've changed over time:

About six months ago, I saw my ex for what I believe will be the last time. For a while we did talk occasionally, but I found that more painful than a complete break. It's finally coming to this point where we don't know each other. He's never seen my new house, and he's never going to see it. He doesn't really know what my life is like anymore. That kind of thing used to make me feel sad—the new stuff that I'm never going to share with him. But lately I've noticed that it doesn't seem to matter anymore. My feelings have lessened and lessened over time, and now it would feel like talking to a stranger.

While there's often some level of sadness that initially accompanies such a break, many women also find it a relief. They see it as freeing to "clean the slate" and start anew.

Though you may embrace the freedom of giving your ex the kiss-off, the fact that a friendship is undesirable or not possible may make you question what this means about you or your old relationship. Lily started to doubt the importance of her former love:

For a while, I felt really bad that we weren't going to be friends. Partially because I'd completely lost this person who was so important to me. But also because there was this voice inside my head that kept saying, "If you can't even be friends with him, what kind of relationship did you have?" I wondered if every one of those four years had been a waste, a sham. But as time went by and I started to move on, I could see that what we had was really important to me. I loved him immensely, and our relationship was important for me. I wouldn't be who I am today without having that experience. And while it ended badly, I want to be able to hold the good times close to me and respect what we had.

This Thing Called Closure

Women who've been through the major changes in a breakup and whose overwhelming feelings of anger, sadness, or loss begin to fade, often find themselves wondering, "When will the postbreakup process finally come to an end?" Even if you and your ex are in new relationships, you may not have experienced a sense of closure around your past relationship.

What is closure, exactly? Well, from our interviews we've discerned that it's not necessarily one definable experience or moment. It's more like a sense that the relationship as it once was is over, as well as an acceptance of what happened in the past and how things are in the present. Closure doesn't necessarily mean we forget about or discard the past. Rather, it's more about accepting our past, integrating it into our present sense of self, and actively moving on towards our future.

Nikki, who is still in the rebuilding phase of her breakup, pointed out that closure isn't about how the relationship itself ends:

I have to keep in mind that closure is not going to be how I want things to end. It's an acceptance of what happened and what I went through.

Closure is a personal experience, based on your own self-reflection. No one can control how or when it will happen. It's a feeling that develops when you've taken the time to examine your past experiences and your feelings about them. Using these insights to make decisions about how you would like future relationships to differ can serve as a bridge to the future, helping to facilitate the closure of your past relationship.

For Jeanette, the road to closure had many stops along the way:

It seems to me that closure happens in stages. First, it's like, "Now is the time when I know that we're never getting back together." Then, "Now is the time when I know that I don't ever want to get back together, and I'm not in love with you anymore." And, "Now is the time when I try to be okay with myself." Then suddenly one day you realize that you're not angry, sad, or feeling a longing for that relationship anymore.

I know without a doubt that I'm better off now than I ever could have been in that relationship, though when I first broke up I never even imagined that I'd really feel this way. I still think about him and our time together, but the feelings aren't as intense as they used to be. I feel that it's essentially closed, a part of my life that I want to remember but that I'd never want to return to.

Like Jeanette, other women experience closure as a slow progression. But is this a linear progression, or is it more like the grief process in its nonlinear nature? Liza's question echoed the sentiments of many of the women we talked to: "Is closure absolute, or does it have a sort of permeable membrane?"

While there isn't a definite answer to this question, it seems likely that, being a part of human nature, closure isn't a definite, absolute finality. Because of this, it can be difficult to distinguish between when closure has actually been achieved and when there's simply a resting period in the grief process. Sarah found that glimpses of closure came and went as feelings of grief were revived:

At times I've felt like I had closure, but then new things come up and those old feelings still spring to life. Whether I really had closure before and this is just leftover stuff I have to deal with, I'm not sure. But if it is closure, it's a different kind than I used to have when I was younger. The kind of pain when I see him or think about him that used to eventually go away at the end of my past relationships, now informs my life. I carry that pain around with me now and it's closer to the surface than it used to be with past lovers. I used to be able to get rid of it or not think about it. And now I think about it a lot. I don't necessarily feel that it's unhealthy. I mean, I used to think that there was something wrong with me for not being able to put it behind me. But now I think it's okay because this breakup was a huge learning experience for me—it really changed my life a lot. So whatever I'm learning from it is still happening.

Sarah's experience mirrors Liza's question about a permeable kind of closure. While you may have an experience or period of time in which you feel you've put the relationship behind you, it's not impossible to have feelings resurface. This is especially true when you run into stumbling blocks, such as finding out that your ex is dating someone new or making a lifetime commitment to a new partner, or your own experience of a life crisis or significant change (we talk about these stumbling blocks more later in this chapter).

Sabine is skeptical about the idea of closure itself, raising the possibility that closure is just a construct that people devise as a way to cope with their emotions, as opposed to an actual experience:

I always think of closure as a pretty little package that you create for yourself so that you can throw your emotions in this box and say, "Okay, I'll tie it up. It's tidy and I'll store it back here."

Most women wish at some point that they could round up all of their feelings and stash them away. However, it is the acceptance and integration of emotions that brings about closure, not a denial or setting aside of them. While we may employ some form of denial while in the ground zero or rebuilding stages, permanently ignoring or locking away feelings only prevents us from comfortably moving on.

Because closure is a personal experience that pertains to internal feelings and perceptions, there's some flexibility in terms of how we can define it. The main criteria for closure is that our feelings have been examined and accepted. But women's experiences of this acceptance varies. Try to pay attention to your own feelings and experiences and honor them.

How Can I Get Some?

While we can't will closure to happen, we can take steps toward it. Julia worked toward closure in the early stage of her breakup by blaming everything on her ex and focusing on all of his bad and annoying traits:

I think it was the only way I could make it permanent in my mind. If I'd let some of the good memories in, I might've allowed myself to get back together with him—and that would've been really bad. So I focused on all the things that were wrong with him and with us.

While this allowed Julia to begin separating herself from the defunct relationship, after a time, this thinking becomes less useful, effectively holding her back instead of helping her progress. When we have successfully and completely put our old relationships away, establishing our own independent lives, we're able to see both the good and bad in the former relationship. Instead of focusing on the negatives qualities of our exes, we're free to see them and the relationship more objectively. This is because, as author Diane Vaughan found, negative definitions, the sort of "ex bashing" so many of us indulge in, is often necessary to the transition away from our partners. When we finally feel secure in our new, postbreakup identities, we can let most of those overly negative perspectives go.

So, in effect, there are different steps that we take throughout the postbreakup process that lead to closure. If we find ourselves unable to let go of our feelings for our exes, focusing on their bad traits can help us make the necessary emotional severing. However, as we enter the settling-in stage, it's time to let go of the past and integrate it into our current self-identity. And the first step of this integration process is acknowledging to ourselves how things really were, from a combined perspective of then and now.

Once Jeanette had a sense of closure she felt ready to revisit her perception of the relationship:

I spent some time forcing myself to think about the good times we'd had and the things about him I'd loved. It was hard at first, because I had really closed that part of myself off in order to protect myself from wanting to get back together or romanticizing the way it used to be. But once I realized that I was happy with my life and that I'd never in a million years want to go back to the life I'd had with him, it felt safe to acknowledge that there were a lot of good things about the past, too.

It was a relief, because for a while there I was really wondering if I'd been crazy to have ever been with him. But seeing the whole picture really cemented for me the fact that I hadn't been wrong to love him, that the relationship was what I'd wanted at the time, that it hadn't been one long mistake. And most importantly, that after acknowledging that to myself, I was still happy and relieved to be moving on.

Revisiting old emotions from the relationship and breakup itself, when we feel ready to do so, can help us achieve an even deeper level of closure. Denise, whose relationship ended when her partner made the decision to move out, talks about her journey towards resolution, and the inevitable pain that accompanies it:

It's never convenient. I always hate it. It feels like forever. It seems almost as bad in the moment as it was in the first few weeks—although it really isn't, I can say that after ten months—but it's just as consuming, if not as intense. But the truth is, if I try not to run from it, it seems not to be as long-lasting.

Lily spent a lot of time obsessing before she finally achieved closure:

One day I was driving home, and I stopped at the stoplight, and I realized that the whole way home I had been thinking of things he had told me and trying to decide if they were true or not. Every waking second, for months and months, that was always in the back of my head. I was always trying to figure it out, like it was a puzzle or something.
But I've finally accepted that I'll never know what really happened—what he really did and what he was really thinking. I'll never know when all of the lies started. I could try and figure it out forever—but it's not worth it to me. It's too exhausting, and in the final analysis, the exact whens and wheres and whys don't change the fact that our relationship is over. And as painful as it was, I really wouldn't change things back to the way they used to be even if I could.

The revisiting and obsessing over the past is one way to work toward closure. As Denise and Lily both experienced, eventually we tire of thinking about the relationship and move to the next level of closure—acceptance.

Many women have the opportunity to work with their ex-lovers to resolve feelings about the relationship and their breakup. Barbara, who maintained a friendship with her ex-partner after the breakup, said:

There was about seven months between when we broke up and when I left for graduate school, so we had a nice chunk of time to reach some sort of closure. We decided to go to therapy together to help with it.

In retrospect we both agree that we broke up in a really good way. We broke up with a lot of respect for each other. But I also think that the therapy really helped. It helped us see that there was a lot of love that was still there and that it didn't need to be a messy breakup.

This mutual commitment to working toward closure together is one that's especially useful to people who wish to remain friends. Barbara's experience allowed her and her ex-lover to detach with minimum resentment and maximum respect and caring.

Other women we talked to had to work on achieving closure mostly on their own, with some eventual help from their ex-lovers. Miranda said:

After a point, I really wanted him to take responsibility for his part in the breakup. He didn't take responsibility for the fact that we'd had, in a lot of ways, a relationship that could've gone in one direction, but at a certain point he just pulled out. I wanted him to take responsibility for his portion of the breakup. Finally he did, and we sat down and talked about it.

This opportunity to speak with an ex, especially when it involves someone taking responsibility or apologizing for hurtful actions, can speed up closure. Unresolved feelings, such as resentment, pain, betrayal, guilt, and rejection, can fester and prolong the postbreakup processing. Having the opportunity to make amends with an ex can be healing for both of you.

The majority of women we spoke to, however, were left with the task of resolving their feelings without any help from their ex-partners. Many women felt that this lack of contact or cooperation was a barrier to achieving closure. Kris said:

I believe in closure, but I don't think I have it. I mean, I don't have an emotional charge around everything now, but it still feels . . . unclosed or hanging. We've had virtually no contact since the breakup. I mean, to have had these five years together and then nothing. I don't have the same strong feelings I had before, but it doesn't feel closed.

When a relationship ends suddenly and you don't have the opportunity to settle things with your ex-lover, getting over the breakup and moving on can feel impossible or insurmountable. Perhaps even more complicated is when an ex maintains that there will be an opportunity to work on closure together when he or she is

ready. Anne's ex-lover converted to the Mormon church and hetero-
sexuality in one week, effectively ending their three-year relationship:

*She told me she was going to tell me exactly why we had broken up,
but she had to talk to her family first. When I asked when, she said,
"Oh, in a week, in a week." So she just keeps prolonging this big
statement she's going to make. In the meantime it's sort of like a wound
turning into a scar. I don't think the relationship will ever actually
close. But there will be, on my part, some getting over it.*

When an ex-partner keeps you waiting for answers, it can be
tempting to put your own emotional growth on hold while you wait.
Some ex-partners may be stalling for time while they figure out what
it is they really feel and want, while others may want to maintain
some kind of contact, resorting to outright manipulation. It's up to
you how long you wait and if you wait at all.

Lynn, whose ex-lover left her to date a mutual friend, also had
the realization that she'd need to work toward closure on her own:

*I just saw her at the beginning of this week, and it was the first
time that I've been able to really just know that there isn't any
intention on her part to communicate with me. That she just wants to
be pleasant and comfortable, and that I'm not going to get anything I
need from her—I'm not going to get resolution from her, it needs to
come from me.*

Lily ended her relationship when she discovered that her ex had
been lying about a variety of things. Since she no longer trusted him,
she decided that it was best for her to minimize contact with him:

*I couldn't trust anything he said anymore anyway. It really reminded
me of "The Boy Who Cried Wolf." Suddenly, even his seemingly most
sincere words were questionable to me. For a long time, maybe a year or
so, I found it so difficult not being able to fully express to him what I
had to say about what happened. I never really got a chance to tell him
off, to express my anger and pain for how he'd knowingly hurt me.*

*But as time went on, I started to deal with it more on my own,
and I eventually reached a place of calm, of acceptance that I'll never
really know his truth and he'll never know mine—and that's fine.
Under the circumstances, I think that was probably for the best,
anyway.*

*A few months ago I got a letter from him, where he was saying, "I
realize that we have all of these unresolved issues, and I'm finally ready*

*to talk to you about things." But now it's like, I don't need to talk it
out with you. I don't have unresolved issues. I've already dealt with it.
You may have issues, but we don't have issues, because there is no
"we" anymore. I knew that I couldn't work it out with him, so I was
sort of forced myself to work it out on my own. And I did it just fine.*

Finding resolution from a breakup on your own can be a daunting task. However, in many circumstances, it's the only option. Lee, a
massage therapist whose lover broke up with her over the phone and
was reluctant to have a face-to-face conversation, had to move herself
toward resolution:

*I tried to bring closure. I wrote him a letter one night that said, "With
all of my heart, I just want to tell you I will make it my goal to always
remember the best times that we've had. I'm blessing you, I'm releasing
you." I tried, I burned sage, I did all the things a massage therapist
knows how to do to cut things off. But there was no reciprocity from
him because he wouldn't agree to meet in person, so I had to do
everything I could do myself to try to find closure.*

If you haven't yet experienced closure, there are several things
you can do to work toward it. Clunis and Green offer a few suggestions: You could decide to create a formal ending by having friends
conduct a closure ceremony for you and your ex, which could give
both you and your former partner the opportunity to voice what was
good and bad in the relationship. You could also take a few days to
go alone to a place that is significant to you and allow yourself to
experience a sort of "cleansing" of the old and initiation of the new.
Or, you could throw yourself a "new beginnings" shower, formally
welcoming this new era in your life.

The women we spoke to had other great ideas to hasten closure.
Nikki made a scrapbook that cataloged her past relationship, allowing her to revisit old memories and fully grieve her losses. Clare
packed up photos and mementos and buried them in a place that had
been significant to her and her partner. Many of the women we
talked to strengthened old friendships and forged new ones, allowing
their revitalized life to give them the strength to face and accept old
emotions. Several of the women said they benefited greatly from
entering therapy. We each get to choose whatever methods we feel
will most benefit us.

Some women, such as Indigo, need to reclaim control of their
lives and set very firm boundaries with their ex-lovers in order to get

closure. Indigo had to first make sure her ex stopped intruding in her life before she could fully put the past behind her:

She lives on the East Coast, and she would check my messages from there. She had the code to my machine. And it happened way more than once. She was just checking to see what was going on in my life. So, I was talking to this friend of mine who just said, "That's totally unacceptable!" And I thought, "Yeah! It is!" So my friend and I traded machines so I could have a machine with a new code. Several times she tried to call and check the messages, and I could hear the numbers being punched in. But I just wasn't going to play anymore. I think that let her know that I wouldn't be messed with anymore. I was done.

Closure is about the resolution of our feelings. It's up to us how we set about achieving it—whether we enter therapy to receive guidance, write unsent letters that express how we feel, talk with our former partners about our feelings, or simply spend time alone and with friends processing and resolving our emotions.

What Does Closure Feel Like?

Sometimes closure brings with it a sense of absolute finality. Based on our interviews, this feeling seems most common when the old relationship was somehow toxic or destructive, or when the breakup involved the intentional infliction of pain. Liza, who hasn't yet experienced closure with her most recent relationship, recalls a past experience of absolute closure:

I've only had closure with the first guy I broke up with, who beat me up. I was like, "Go ahead, kill yourself! I don't care. Just stop coming here!" That's closure!

In Liza's case, closure served to protect her from being further abused, and it entailed the breaking of all contact with her ex.

Maria experienced a sort of reconciliation with her ex-partner that allowed her to achieve the peace of closure:

There was an incident when, maybe four years ago, she came to me to apologize for the pain she had inflicted upon me. She brought a gift that was very significant. She brought me a Tibetan thanka that we'd had a big fight over when we were traveling. She was supposedly buying this thanka as a present for me, then she ended up keeping it. And it caused this really bad feeling. So one day she came and she brought me this thanka as a way of her asking for forgiveness. She said that she knew she had been very hurtful to a lot of people, and that the person she hurt most was me. She said she'd never intended it, and she apologized. And that really, really closed it. Since then I've felt a calm about that relationship.

Many of the women we talked to spoke of a desire for their ex to apologize, to take responsibility for their part in the ending of the relationship. The women who did eventually receive this resolution with their partners found it immensely freeing.

Other women, like Clare, had specific moments of closure, times in which they were reminded of the forward movement in their lives:

He had given me a "promise ring," an engagement ring, really. When we broke up, I took it off. Then, I was sitting with my friend at the end of the summer, and I looked at my hand and realized that the tan line from the ring was gone.

Clare's physical "proof" of her relationship faded over time, just as her emotional attachments disintegrated as she moved on with her life.

Simone doesn't feel she's experienced complete closure yet, but she has had experiences that she sees as steps towards resolution:

I had saved some of my answering machine tapes with messages from my ex on them. I saved some of them because they meant so much to me at the time. And I'm glad I did, because when everything started to go bad I could listen to these tapes and know that at some point he really did care about me. So, a couple of days ago, my friend was over and I started playing one of the tapes. My friend said, "Is this upsetting you? Is this too soon to be listening to this?" And I said, "No." I wasn't upset. I was disconnected from it.

This temporary feeling of disconnection allows Simone to take a breather from the work of accepting what happened in her relationship. Having taken a step past grief-filled ground zero, she can begin to imagine how her life will be once she has achieved closure, and this gives her the incentive to continue working through her feelings in order to achieve complete resolution.

As all of these women's stories demonstrate, there is no one way to feel closure. Some women have sudden moments in which they realize that they are no longer troubled by the past and are now enjoying the present and looking forward to their future. Others, like Maria, have a conversation with their ex-partners that eases their hurt and allows them to move on. You may experience closure as a gradual lessening or a sudden transformation, a permanent resolution or a permeable and ever-shifting change in feeling.

What's in It for Me?

Achieving closure is hard work. Sometimes denial seems like an easier route. Other times it's tempting to cover emotions from the past with new relationships and experiences, rather than confronting them directly. This can work for a time. But if you allow yourself to find true resolution, you'll achieve a new sense of self that's founded on strength, power, and self-determination. And as long as you're working in the right direction, you don't have to wait for complete closure to enjoy these benefits—they're waiting for you all along the way.

Clare and her partner broke up a few months before a big move that they had planned to make together. Once on her own, Clare decided to go anyway:

After moving out to Baltimore by myself, now I can think about moving to New York or New Orleans, and it's no problem. Whereas, if he had moved with me out to Baltimore, I would still have been scared to do things like that alone.

By seizing her independence and conquering her fears, Clare has opened up new possibilities. She could have decided not to go, as some of those around her suggested. Instead, she forged ahead, proving to herself and to others that she wasn't going to remain stuck in the past—she was going to continue moving toward the future. This was a crucial step toward the closure she later experienced. She believes that this new sense of self and closure go hand in hand:

I actually think I have closure now, and the really cool thing is that it has nothing really to do with him at all. It has to do with me—being myself, who I am, what I'm doing now, for me. I think that's when you reach closure—when you're perfectly happy with yourself.

I had this amazing dream that I'll never forget. In the dream, I was sleeping in the desert, and it was just before the sun came up. It was still dark, and I thought, "Where am I?" I was sleeping on the ground in a sleeping bag. The sun started coming up, and I realized that I was in the desert. I saw all these rolling hills and dunes. And, because the sun was just coming up, the hills were all golden colored.

All of a sudden I could hear horses' hooves on the ground, so I got up and got out of the way. All of these horses with riders on them went by. I was waving to them, saying, "See you later!" Then one of them started slowing down. He was looking at me, though he didn't say anything. It was like he was worried about me. So I said to him, "I'm okay. You can go." And he turned around and rode off. And the sky was an amazing red and then blue color. And, when I woke up, I realized how much I was looking forward to my future, by myself.

No Turning Back?

Does achieving closure mean that you'll have it forever? What happens if your ex happens to slide back into your life, and you discover that you'd really like to give a romantic relationship with him or her a second try? Does that mean that you've "failed" at closure? If you have no plans whatsoever of going back to your ex you may think that you'll never have to worry about this issue. But, you never know what lies in the future, and you may find examining the permanence of closure valuable. Sarah raised the issue of closure and getting back together with an ex-partner:

It's so interesting to me that people get together again after they've been separated. What kind of closure must they have had? Did they really say good-bye to one another, forget about each other, then run into each other again when circumstances were such that they wanted to have a relationship again? Or did they leave a door open to that originally? I don't know the answer, but I think things just become a little less cut-and-dried the more serious relationships you have. I think closure becomes a different thing.

While a few of the women we spoke to did reunite with their partners (which we'll discuss further in chapter 7), the implicit question regarding closure that Sarah raises is: If you'd like to get back together, but it isn't currently possible; can you achieve closure? Or does the desire to reunite prohibit complete closure?

There are no absolute answers to these questions. But through talking to the women we interviewed, we've come to believe that closure is about your own acceptance of the past and the integration of your past self with your present self. This process doesn't actually involve your ex—you don't need anyone else to help you make your own peace with your breakup. When thinking of it this way, it makes sense that you can have closure and still get back together, because it's the past relationship that you've put behind you, not necessarily your present relationship with your ex.

As you go through your postbreakup process, your feelings may change about the idea of reuniting with your ex. Some of the women we talked to used the possibility of getting back together to comfort them throughout the initial rough stages of the breakup, letting go of this possibility when it no longer appealed to them. One of the women we spoke to who later married her ex said that she'd thought the breakup was permanent, and that it was only later that she reopened the possibility. If you feel you can achieve closure—an acceptance of the past and its integration with your present—while still leaving the door open for a future reunion with your ex, then feel free to do so if you choose. As long as you aren't pining for the past and preventing yourself from moving forward, closure isn't an impossibility.

When Your Ex Dates Again and Other Stumbling Blocks

There will inevitably be some stumbling blocks that temporarily delay your progress. These stumbling blocks might be pebbles, making you pause for a few hours or days, or boulders, requiring a combination of elbow grease and creativity to surpass. Anything that pulls you uncontrollably back into old feelings can be a stumbling block—seeing old friends, running in to your ex, having a personal crisis, or finally achieving something that you'd worked toward with your ex in the past.

One of the most common stumbling blocks the women we spoke to experienced was when they found out their ex-partners had started seeing someone new or made a lifetime commitment to a new partner. It was especially difficult for women who were still in the ground zero or rebuilding stages. Clare's ex started dating someone new within weeks of their breakup:

When I first got the e-mail he sent me, telling me he was seeing someone else, I was sitting in the computer lab at school, and I just started sobbing. I went back to my apartment building, sat on the steps, and cried.

When you've barely had a chance to pick up the pieces, it's difficult to hear that your ex has moved on to the next relationship. It can feel like a further rejection or another dose of humiliation. If your ex leaves you specifically for another person, you may be so shocked that you respond in ways you'd have never thought you would. When Lynn found out that her partner was seeing one of their friends, her reaction surprised her:

I was saying, "Maybe we can both date you." I was so far gone. It was so psychotic. I had not one shred of self-respect left.

Since she doesn't have contact with her partner, Lily doesn't know whether he's dating new people yet or not. But for the first year or so after her breakup, she still wondered about it, and she had emotional responses to all of her imagined scenarios:

When I thought about him by himself, I felt sorry for him. But when I thought about him with someone else, I hated him. I really think it had to do with how I felt about myself. Like, if you're with someone, you're okay, and you're moving on. But if you don't have someone new, then you're not. Which is total bullshit! But there was a part of me that still bought into that, and I had to retrain myself to think differently.

Lily found it helpful to think about her feelings and ask herself why she thought she was responding in a given way. Whether you have no feelings at all or are overwhelmed with grief, anger, and humiliation, you can learn a lot about your beliefs by examining your responses. From there, you can decide what you'd like to change.

Julia was creeped out when her ex started dated someone she knew:

My ex's new girlfriend was a friend of mine. We'd been friends for a while, and we'd even lived together a few years back—actually it was when Jake and I started going out. She was there for all of it, witnessed the whole thing, was there for all of the horrible things that Jake and I went through together at the beginning of our relationship, and she knew all of the shitty things he'd said to me. And then I found out that about six months ago they started going out. I was just like, "Ew, this is so wrong. You were a part of this on my side." And every once in a while I'll remember something else she knew about our sex life or something like that, and I'll just say, "Yuck."

When your ex starts dating someone you once trusted and confided in, it can feel like a double betrayal.

Another twist on this situation is when your ex starts dating someone who seems, at least superficially, to be a lot like you. Clare said:

His new girlfriend is a white woman, and a redhead, but still she's a lot like me. I mean, she has the same haircut I had when Pete and I met, she wears the same glasses that I do, and her mannerisms are like mine.

Especially when your ex is the one who decided to end your relationship, it can be disconcerting to feel like he or she has gone out looking for your virtual twin. It can cause you to wonder: Why didn't my ex just stick with me?

Lucy's ex ended up dating and recently marrying the woman he confided in during his breakup with Lucy:

When I heard about it I felt sick to my stomach. I knew that they were good friends and that she was comforting him during our breakup, and although I was breaking up with him, I still felt like, "Robert, I'm your soul mate, remember? Don't just fall madly in love right now."

It has nothing to do with wanting to get back together with him. It's just this part of me that loved him, that still feels connected to him in some way. It was just weird to hear that he'd gotten married, because it's like some kind of final closure. It's like, "That's it. We're going to live this life out and die separately, and that's that." Which maybe would have been fine with me if he'd been single, I don't know.

Regardless of who your ex is with, whether it's a stranger or someone you know, it can affect you. Miranda said:

I just found out last week that Everett's getting married. Every time I think I'm past the whole breakup thing, there's another mark, another part of closure, and this is a major one.

Of course, there are different degrees of dating and relationships. You may be unaffected when your ex goes out on a first date, but what about when he or she falls in love? Hannah, who is still close friends with her ex, said:

At first, Scott didn't seem to like his new girlfriend much. He would talk about her really casually. Than, after a while, it changed, and he didn't talk about her as much. Meanwhile, I was getting closer to my new partner, but it was hard, 'cause I still felt linked to Scott. So, one day I asked Scott if he was in love with Toni. And he said, "Yes." They'd only been seeing each other for two months. In some way I had known what he was going to say, and I'd forced him to say it—because I wanted to try and break that hold. And at first it was fine to hear it, but gradually I got more and more angry and depressed. I was furious with him for being "in love" with someone after two months, after our huge breakup.

Why does it affect you when your ex dates someone new? Hannah shared why it was so hard for her:

It's almost like, if they're with someone new, it denigrates what you had. "How can you love someone new when we were in love?!" But there's no connection between the two anymore—it just feels like there is.

Julia realized that one of the crucial factors in determining how big of a stumbling block her ex's new partnership was for her was how happy she was in her own life:

As my current relationship started to sour and I was hearing more about Jake and his new relationship and how much time they were spending together and how she met the family, I started feeling a little disturbed and thinking, "I'm not happy anymore. He can't be either."

Renee, whose partner left her for another woman, knows that hearing of an ex-partner's new relationship isn't always just about pain—sometimes there's a subtle undertone of sweet justice:

The last time we had a friendly, sociable time together, she told me over brunch that her new partner was having a really bad time with menopause and wasn't responding well to the drugs, and actually liked gin an awful lot, and was something of an abusive drunk, and that they were moving to New Orleans in August. I sat there and I swear, I didn't crack a smile, I didn't. But I thought, "You're moving to the murder capital of the United States, in the hottest month, with a woman who's an abusive drunk having a really bad menopause—thank you, Jesus!"

Locking Up the Storage Space

So you reach some sort of closure and navigate around or over, or bulldoze through, the stumbling blocks that are in your path. And you take your past and put it into storage—there for you to take out whenever you want to reminisce, but no longer underfoot in your everyday life. Now what?

Well, now you can shift into high gear and really immerse yourself in your present and future. It's finally time to move in and move on.

Chapter 7

Moving In,
Moving On

At first, I put all of my energy into getting over my breakup and reconnecting with my friends. But now that my life is back on track, I've started really reaching out to new people. It's a little scary sometimes, putting myself out there. But I know that in order to keep growing, I've got to continue adding to my existing community.

—Lily

The idea of a date is such a weird social construct, where you both sort of agree that you'll sit and talk and get to know each other, and maybe later you'll make out.

—Hannah

I am no longer willing to put up with someone loving parts of me. I love all of me, and whoever I'm with in the future must do the same. I realize that I am worth so much—my self-image has shot through the roof. I won't compromise myself anymore.

—Joy

Part of the settling-in process is enjoying the community we've built around ourselves and continuing to reach out—working hard to add new and varied members to our existing community. This outreach includes continuing to meet new friends, maintaining strong relationships with old friends and family, and perhaps taking steps to reenter the romantic domain. It's the time to enjoy the benefits of the work we've done rebuilding and to reinvest ourselves in our new lives.

Make New Friends, but Keep the Old

As the postbreakup experience progresses, we become more confident and self-sufficient. This stronger sense of self is reflected in the fostering of our friendships. By the end of the process, we will have rebuilt lives that better meet our individual needs (Radford et al. 1997).

Those friendships that have withstood the postbreakup turmoil and have made it to the settling-in stage are probably pretty stable. These are the people who've stuck by you through the breakup, helping you heal and celebrating with you as you began to feel better. The important players in your life right now are probably people you'll want to maintain close connections to as you settle in to your new life. Marilyn talked about how important these people still are to her:

I found my friends and community during our breakup, and I've maintained those relationships over the years. I still have a sense of intimacy with the women who were single moms with me, and the former neighbors who were there when the kids were sick or when I needed a cup of coffee and a break. The connections I made when I was most vulnerable remain the most dear to me.

One drawback to the settling-in stage is that, now that the crisis is over, it can be easy to slip back into the habit of taking your friends for granted. It takes a conscious effort to keep your relationships strong and vital. Jeanette said:

With the new friends I've been making, the new projects I've taken on, the time I finally realize I need to myself, it seems like I have a lot less space in my life. I'm still struggling to achieve some semblance of balance. It's really hard not to put my old friends on the back burner, because I know they're there for me and they love me. But the single most important thing my breakup taught me was that I need to be vigilant about putting energy into my most cherished relationships. My friends are my lifeline.

In addition to maintaining existing friendships, it's also important to continue adding new people to your life after the settling-in stage. Lily said:

At first, I put all of my energy into getting over my breakup and reconnecting with my friends. But now that my life is back on track, I've started really reaching out to new people. It's a little scary sometimes, putting myself out there. But I know that in order to keep growing, I've got to continue adding to my existing community.

Unpack Your Baggage

The prospect of entering into another committed relationship—or even just dating casually—may raise fear in your heart, especially if you haven't finished dealing with all the baggage you're carrying from your past relationship and its demise. Perhaps you get along just fine in your everyday, single life, but you worry that opening yourself up to the possibility of love would expose wounds that are only partially healed. Most of the women we spoke to were at least a little nervous about getting close to someone new, because emotional intimacy requires a level of vulnerability and trust that can be hard to muster after a painful split. If the thought of a new love utterly terrifies you, you may have to unpack a little more of the emotional baggage you carry.

Some of this baggage may be much older than you'd imagine. A breakup, just like any other significant loss, has the potential to exacerbate core issues developed earlier in your life. Some of the women we interviewed talked about how their new partnerships forced them to really work through their deep-seated issues. Hannah discovered that she was much more sensitive in her new relationship than she ever thought she'd be, and it took her a while to figure out why:

After I left Scott, I thought I'd recovered really well. I was happy and relieved to be away from that relationship. But when I got together with Michael, I had the strangest experiences of depression. He could say or do the smallest things, tiny things that I would interpret as rejection, and I would just crash. My reaction was so over the top that it forced me to think about just exactly why I was so upset. I finally realized that Scott's rejection of me—by not wanting to get married—was triggering old, bad feelings about my dad abandoning me. I was so sensitive at this point that Michael just had to look at me funny and I was plunged into the depths of despondency. It was so hard for both me and Michael to understand, but it was all old unresolved stuff echoing into my new relationship.

It can be tempting to try to avoid facing painful core issues that were stirred up by our breakups, especially if we feel pretty good in general. But, as Hannah found, these unresolved feelings can complicate our relationships with new loves and make us react to things in ways that seem boggling even to ourselves.

You may find that embarking on a new relationship can be therapeutic, allowing you to encounter and deal with unresolved issues you may not have been aware of. You may be able to start busting through those barriers and experimenting with intimacy again in a new relationship, but it may be a tough job. Wendy said:

I've been dating Eric for almost a year now, and it's only in the last two months that I feel like I'm really opening up. It's been like pulling teeth, because he's very shy, and I've been totally closed and overprotective. I've just been sending messages of "You'd better back off." So it's been tiny, tiny little baby steps. And in terms of sex, I thought I could just start swinging right away, and it just didn't work that way. All my assumptions were shot to hell and I really had to face up to things. I couldn't use all of my old tricks and I couldn't manipulate him—I'd lost all of my old games somewhere along the way. I actually think giving up those strategies is good, but when I figured out how hard it would be, it sure threw me for a loop. Opening up like that was just like sticking my thumb into my gut and ripping it open.

Several of the women we spoke to felt the need to examine their feelings in further depth before they ventured out again into the dating world. Lynn talked about how her ex's deception left her with trust issues that she needs to at least partially deal with before she can open up to anyone new:

I can't imagine even contemplating trusting somebody. I feel like I'd be a complete handful. I'd feel like any nice thing would be cause for suspicion—because that was the thing, she was very nice, she was very sweet, so a lot of my anger is attached to her not meaning those nice and sweet things. So how's that going to happen? If they say something nice, I'm going to think, "Right. You're probably just a bitch and you just don't want to tell me what you really think." I think there's a lot of work I can do before I can actually trust someone new, but I still think that the only time that some of it's going to come up is when my heart starts to open. But there's going to be some amount of terror about being vulnerable—and I just have to know that.

Opening up can be scary, but a lot of that fear can be alleviated by trying to work through your issues before new romance comes into the picture. But, as Lynn points out, it's unreasonable to expect yourself to be "issue free" when you embark on a new relationship. Jeanette said:

When Chris and I first broke up, I was terrified of being alone. It took me a good long while before I felt comfortable with the single me. And I've spent this time in therapy, really focusing on myself and the things that hold me back in life. I've grown tremendously. But now that I understand what happened in my last relationship and I'm feeling pretty confident that I won't make the same exact mistakes as I did before, a new fear has come up: I'm starting to feel scared of the idea of entering into a new relationship. I'm terrified of losing my independence, my self-sufficiency, my identity as a single woman. I think it's because I was too merged in my last relationship, and now I'm a complete, individual unit. But I've never been complete and shared my life with someone. So I guess that's the next step, though I have to admit that just thinking about it sort of freaks me out.

As Lynn and Jeanette both point out, there may be a point at which a new love can push you to grow further than you can alone. It may be unreasonable to expect that you'll enter any relationship completely baggage-free, though you probably don't want to bring along a U-haul full of unresolved issues. Perhaps you can instead strike a realistic balance and just have a few carry-on pieces.

Flying Solo

Many of the women we spoke to were enjoying the single life and were planning to keep it that way, at least for a while. Especially if you haven't reached a feeling of closure on your past relationship, you may find that spending time alone can give you the space to figure things out and decide how you want future relationships to be. Lynn talked about the reasons behind her decision to remain single:

Staying single was the best decision I made. It's been hard not to seek the comfort of a relationship, but I don't want to repeat what has happened. So until I'm feeling clear and sure of my feelings, I'll just continue to thrive as a single person.

Romantic partnerships demand compromise. Once you settle in and begin enjoying your newly rebuilt life, you may find that you want to enjoy the fruits of your labor for a while before delving back into the land of serious give-and-take. Elizabeth talked about the independence her single status was allowing her:

I'm choosing to remain single for a while, and I'm finding it a very positive choice. As heartbroken as I was after the breakup, I've really liked being single and focusing on my own life. I've moved from the Deep Suburbs (where I lived with my ex) to a central urban location with lots of lesbians, so my social life has picked up a lot. I'm focusing mainly on building a community for myself, and I don't want to turn my attention away from that to a new romantic relationship.

Also, I like being able to make my own decisions without having to consult anyone. I had to compromise so much in my relationship, and I love being able to make spontaneous decisions. It does get lonely, too, but I'm coping with that, and I don't feel lonely all the time. I love my new apartment, I love being near everything, and I love living by myself.

Dating can take quite a bit of time and energy. Like many of the women we interviewed, Denise would rather continue to reap the benefits from branching out in other aspects of her life, rather than shift her focus to the romantic realm:

I used to think that I'd never want to be single. But now I'm finding out that I love being single. Maybe someday I'll be in a committed relationship again, but I do see things differently now, in terms of my sense of spirituality, my relationship with my children. I could not have fathomed what was available to me from my previous perspective, because I did relationships in a way that was very merged, very coupled, and that was all that mattered.

I have more friends than I've ever had. I'd had a few close friends, and they were lucky if they heard from me from time to time. Now I have several friends I see or talk to on a regular basis. I spend a lot more time alone. I participate much more in the lives of my children. We spend the whole day together, whereas before we might have spent just a piece of a day together. And just the quality of my relationship with the kids—I'm much more present, I spend more time with them, and our relationship is much more intense.

Living single can be liberating, though it may force you to contend with internal and external pressure originating from the couple culture we live in. Daniel Levinson explains:

In the traditional cultural meanings of gender, it is a profound failure for a woman not to become a wife and mother. A "spinster" is discriminated against, subtly and not so subtly, in work organizations, in informal community life, and in social circles composed chiefly of married couples. She is subject to harsh images of the cold ruthless competitor, the needy woman in search of matrimony, the pathetic woman leading an emotionally empty life. (326)

Even if we reject our culture's fear and disapproval of strong, single women, we may find ourselves subconsciously falling into its trappings. Jeanette talked about how she experienced pressure to become recoupled:

It'd been about a year since the breakup, and even though I was still working through things, I started to feel like I should be dating—like there was a time limit to how long it was okay to be single. Also, people were starting to ask me more and more what was going on in my love life, and I felt strange having nothing to tell them. So I went out with a couple of people, and the dates went okay—no horror stories, we just didn't connect.

This feeling went on for a couple of months, leading up to this party my friend and I were having. She was bringing her new boyfriend, and I felt uncomfortable at the thought of being there alone. I was telling another friend about it, and she said, "Sounds like you feel like you should be dating; but do you want to date right now?" I realized in talking with her that actually I was far from ready. So I ended up going to the party alone, and I felt a lot more confident about it. It felt good to know I was alone by choice, and that I was okay with that. Since then, I've really taken to this identity as a strong, independent single woman—it's really liberating.

The Dating Game

The women we spoke to started dating at various points in the post-breakup process—ground zero, rebuilding, or settling in—with varying degrees of success. After getting out of a seven-year relationship, Hannah found that even the concept of dating seemed a little strange:

We were sitting at dinner, sort of uncomfortably eyeballing the menu, and it just struck me as so odd and formal. I asked him, "So, are we on a real date?" I think it sort of flustered him, but he knew what I meant. The idea of a date is such a weird social construct, where you both sort of agree that you'll sit and talk and get to know each other, and maybe later you'll make out. The formality of it just wigged me out.

It's no secret that dating can be hard. Even though it consists primarily of experimentation and learning about another person, it can also be seen as a sort of audition. That's one reason why even the mention of dating can make some postbreakup women run for cover. Zoë felt comfortable in the life she'd constructed after her breakup, but the thought of sitting down to a first date made her more than a little uneasy:

I remember when my friend who set us up called and told me David would be calling me that night. I'd rented a movie and was watching it in the living room when the phone rang. I was paralyzed. I felt like my back was welded to the couch. I listened to his voice as he left a message on the machine and thought, "Oh shit! Now I have to call him back!" And this was someone I really liked!

The idea of venturing out on that first date with someone, checking him or her out, and getting checked out, can make you feel anything from shyness to stark terror. The extremity of your emotional reaction may indicate how emotionally ready you are to get back into the dating pool. If you can't contemplate going out on a date without feeling queasy, you may not be ready. But don't underestimate the normal feelings of nervousness tied in to the dreaded first date.

Wendy thought she was perfectly fine with dating—until she got to the restaurant:

There we were, sitting at a tiny table in this lovely little restaurant, and suddenly I discovered that I was so nervous that I had no appetite whatsoever. I ordered, and when they brought the food, I just continued

*to drink like a fish and chatter on relentlessly, until he was done with
his food. It was so embarrassing to look down at my plate and realize I
hadn't touched my food and I hadn't given him a chance to get a word
in edgewise. Bleah.*

Most of the women we spoke to had some degree of nervousness when they first started dating again. If you find your knees
knocking in terror, try to remember that you're in good company,
and that it does get easier with practice.

And what about that whole idea of dating someone on the
rebound? Many of the women we spoke to found their first attempts
at dating thwarted by unresolved feelings from their breakups. Liza's
friend was hoping their relationship could evolve into something
more, but she found that she couldn't take him up on his offer of
romance:

*A friend of mine, Matt, has been there in the wings forever, the entire
relationship. He's this fabulous, wonderful guy. He would treat me like
a queen. I tried, but I just can't do it. My whole body image is shot.
My self-image is very low, I'm very low. So I tried to explain it to him;
"Matt, I'm just not into anything with you right now. I'm trying to
get over this big hurt over here, and trying to build something with you
just isn't working."*

When Renee's relationship ended, she decided to go after one of
the women she'd been attracted to during her relationship. She
talked about the perils of dating on the rebound:

*I waited about three weeks to call the first one. The image I use is,
there I am, walking with this giant hole in my chest, and going, "You'll
fit! Come 'ere." She woke up one morning and went, "Oh, my God,
what have I gotten myself involved in? I can't do this right now." And
I said, "Whaddaya mean you can't do it? You're perfect. You fit right
here!" We've actually salvaged a wonderful friendship out of that, but it
was a little rocky for a while.*

Daphne talked about two of her postbreakup flings:

*One of my ex's friends just started pursuing me. And I needed the
company. I didn't particularly find this woman attractive, but she was
giving me all of this flattering attention, and I just went to bed with
her one night. It was good at the time, but I regretted it later. And I
did have this other fling, but I wasn't able to give this woman a real*

relationship, and I felt bad about that. I felt really scared to get into
something serious.

Interestingly, many of the women we spoke to talked of dating before they were ready or having flings while they were still trying to get over their ended relationships. While this complicated matters for the majority of these women, there were no huge disasters to speak of. Perhaps this is an indication of how difficult it is to distinguish between normal dating jitters and dating too soon. There are rarely clear distinctions in matters of the heart. The good news, however, is that even those who had regrets about their first excursions into the dating world remained relatively unscathed.

A few of the women we spoke to said that dating gave them just what they needed. Elizabeth talked about her first attempt at dating after her breakup:

I didn't want to date anyone for the first few months, but then, as my
thirtieth birthday approached, I decided I wanted to spend that day with
someone. So I put in a personal ad (which is how I met my ex,
incidentally), got some responses, and ended up having a lovely four- or
five-month fling with a great woman.

Clare also had a positive experience on her first venture out:

I had this summer fling with a friend of mine before I went back to
school. He wasn't someone I'd have wanted to commit to in the long
run, but it was nice to be with someone new. It gave me a chance to
just have fun, without having to negotiate all of the things that come
up when you're entering into a relationship.

While she was still in ground zero, Rachel talked about how she plans to approach dating when she's ready:

I'm not sure I'll ever be interested in deliberately and consciously
"dating." I've always met girlfriends by doing social things with lesbian
groups. I find it easier to meet women that way, rather than specifically
trying to get dates or going to "singles mingles" or whatever. That stuff
is too anxiety-provoking. Besides, I find that when I'm focused on my
interests and on making new friends, I eventually meet women where
there's some sparks, and then it develops into a romance. So whenever
I'm ready for that I'll be open to it, but I don't think I'll make this big
decision to start "girlfriend shopping." I'll just keep doing things the
way I'm doing them now, but I'll be more open to romantic connections.

Not Like Sex with Your Ex

Many of the women we interviewed found that their ideas about sex—and their sexual experiences—changed dramatically after their breakup. It can be startling to discover how different sex can be with a new lover. Clare said:

Pete was the first person I'd ever been with, but, truth be told, he just wasn't a very good lover. I loved him a lot and I found him really attractive, but even without having slept with anyone else I could tell he was lacking in the sex department. So when my friend Craig and I fell into bed together one night about a year after my breakup, it was a huge surprise to find that he was an amazing lover. I wasn't in love with him, he wasn't even my type physically, but the sex was fantastic. And the best part was that he was much more responsive than Pete, which let me know that I wasn't so bad in bed myself. It was a great ego boost.

Sarah found that it took her a long time after her breakup to feel as open to her lovers as she'd been before:

The very first time it was exhilarating, but soon after it became upsetting. I missed my ex, he was a fabulous lover. It was only recently, all of these years later, that I really let go in a way that felt reminiscent of my old relationship. Afterwards I cried for a long time.

Eden saw sex with new lovers as a way to put distance between her and her ex:

I was so obsessed with "scoring" and proving that I was a free agent. I felt like I had to make up for lost time. Since my sex life with my ex had been hampered by bad feelings between us, I was eager to be with someone new, someone who would appreciate me, someone who didn't have a million issues with me. I thought that the best way to put distance between my ex and myself was to have a lot of sex with other people, and do it quickly.

Wendy discovered that she couldn't assume sex with someone new would be as easy as it had been with her ex:

I really thought that I could just jump into bed with this new man and voila, have a great roll in the hay. I thought I "knew" what to do, sexually, to enjoy myself. And I do know. But, for me, it's more than that. I discovered that I have to sort of get to know someone sexually, develop some intimacy and create new patterns with them before I can really get into sex with them. I knew my old lover by heart, so of course sex with him had been pretty easy. But, I found that that ease didn't necessarily translate to someone new. Bummer, huh?

Looking for Love . . . Again

After a relationship has ended, we have the opportunity to look back and examine it with the clarity of hindsight. We may see ways that we acquiesced to our partners or the relationship itself that we now regret. Or we may see some of our own actions as mistakes we'd rather not repeat. While we can't change our past decisions, we can change our expectations for future relationships.

Sarah talked about how she wants her new self-awareness to affect her future relationships:

I wish I'd known that you can't change people in a relationship; I wish I'd trusted my instincts. I want to be able to accept that that other person isn't going to change just because we're in a relationship, and I want to stay more true to myself within the relationship.

When Joy's partner ended their relationship partially on the basis of their twenty-year age difference, Joy change her requirements for potential partners:

I am no longer willing to put up with someone loving parts of me. I love all of me, and whoever I'm with in the future must do the same. I realize that I am worth so much—my self-image has shot through the roof. I won't compromise myself anymore.

Renee has applied her postbreakup knowledge and formed positive expectations for her next love: "I've learned to look for people who pursue joy, have a light within them, and bring you light. " Maria talked about how her new self-knowledge changed the way she was in her next relationship and the kind of partnership she was looking for:

I'm just a lot more emotionally independent. I'd always been in relationships before with people who were older than I was, and when I got into relationships with them, they were emotionally much more together. I looked for security—emotional security. They ended up falling apart a lot more than I would've thought. But from the time I got into those relationships until the height of those relationships, I was looking up to them. They were my stability and my safety. And I think I was ready to get into a relationship with my new partner because she didn't fit that pattern. She's younger; she was unbelievably shy when I met her. So I knew that I couldn't look to her for my emotional guidance. Now I feel so much more self-reliant.

The more self-awareness we take away from our breakup experiences, the better equipped we'll be to avoid patterns that haven't worked for us in the past. This can allow us to make decisions from a more stable and thoughtful place.

Liza talked about how she planned to take a different approach the next time she went looking for love:

I wish I had taken stock early on in the relationship and said to myself, "Wait. Is this what I really want?" I want to be more conscious of what I'm doing, rather than just being swept away.

Miranda has decided to ask potential partners early in the relationship if they have the same values as her:

Now I feel like when I do get in another relationship, I'm going to be really up front: "I don't want to marry you now, but I'm into marriage." It's not a demanding thing or a needy thing, it's like, "I know what I want."

Denise also has specific requirements for her next partnership:

My son is biracial, partially African American. Race would be an enormous factor for me in terms of the next person I might be intimately involved in, because I want my son to feel very loved and respected.

Some of the women we talked to felt that their new relationships benefited from what they'd learned from their breakups. Hannah talked about how she felt her new relationship was in some ways more mature than the one she'd left:

When I first started dating Scott, we were pretty young and unsure of our place in life. After we graduated from college, we sort of clung together for safety from the menace of the adult world. We were pretty dependent on each other in some ways. But with Michael, we were both independent adults. And I think that whole people coming together can build a better life together than two people trying to compensate for their weaknesses by pairing up.

In addition to what we are looking for in a prospective partner, many of us change the way that we want to interact with our lovers. Especially if you've spent time living single, it can be daunting to think about the compromise required in a relationship. Eden talked about how she was able to give and take when she reunited with her ex, while maintaining much clearer boundaries than she had in the past incarnation of their relationship:

I had to be realistic and admit what I had to give up in terms of total autonomy. You have to be responsible to the relationship, you have to be accountable, you have to be considerate. But you can also insist on having a certain amount of independence and focus on yourself, as much as you possibly can. I think there's room for both of those things in relationships, as long as the relationship is healthy and as long as it's been negotiated.

It can be hard to strike a balance of how much to compromise in a relationship. Julia found that in her next relationship, she went from one extreme to another:

Jake was my first real long-term relationship, so I was thinking, "I'm going to be this really strong, independent woman." And then basically I just wilted: "Whatever you want to do. It's okay. It doesn't matter what I want to do. Okay." So when I started going out with Noah, I was like, "No. This is what I want to do, and I don't care what you want to do." I definitely went to the opposite extreme, and I have to relearn how to compromise.

Many of the women we spoke to thought they'd figured out exactly what sort of person they wanted simply by choosing qualities that are the opposite of their ex-partner's. Lucy found herself looking for her ex's opposite, finding a person who did not necessarily meet all of her needs:

I think when I got involved with John I was really horrified by all of the intimacy I was having with Robert. I wasn't ready for it. So I purposely chose John because he was more intellectual than emotional. But sometime into my relationship with Robert, I started wishing he could be a little more emotional.

Whether it's about who we want to see or what we're willing to give up in a relationship, making decisions in a reactionary way may not always serve us, as it can limit our scope of available choices. Jeanette said: "I'm trying to base my judgment of new people on what I really want from my relationships, instead of just trying to avoid what hurt me in the past."

Some of the women we spoke to had already found a new love. We asked them what it was like when they decided to go ahead and throw their hearts into the ring once again and try out another committed relationship. Hannah said:

When I began to fall in love with Michael, I experienced the weirdest sensation of sadness. Instead of just this joyous feeling of being newly in love, it was mixed with this strange sense of sadness at the loss of Scott. It was as if, looking at this new, wonderful man who wanted to make a commitment to me and whom I loved deeply, I was saying a sort of final good-bye to my old relationship, acknowleging that it had ultimately failed. It felt like shutting the door on the past for good.

Second Time Around?

So you go through all this breakup rigmarole—move out, build a new life for yourself, maybe even see other people. But what if you and your ex both realize that, in the end, you still want to be together?

Especially in the early stages of a breakup, fantasies of getting back together, of ending the pain you feel in those early days, can be very appealing. But possibilities of reunion can occur all along the breakup process, especially if you're still close with your ex. And while it may feel strange to consider starting over again with your ex, the ultimate nature of human relationships is fluid, allowing for endless permutations and surprises. Author Diane Vaughan explains that although there are identifiable patterns for uncoupling, this does not mean that these patterns will always play out. Assuming that a breakup is irreversible denies us our power to reconstruct our lives in the way we desire.

A few of the women we interviewed had reunited with their partners. Eden talked about her reasons for getting back together with her ex:

After a year of separation, we did get back together. Even though I spent an entire year cultivating a strong dislike of him, I found that I still really loved only him, and that I didn't want anyone else. When we saw each other after a year, the chemistry between us was still incredibly strong. I think our hiatus helped to confirm our feelings for each other. We needed time and distance to find our own ways, but when we came back to each other, we were more resolved to be better to each other and the relationship. Tomorrow we'll celebrate our four-year wedding anniversary, and to this day I still credit our breakup for our strong, enduring marriage.

Marilyn also credited her breakup ten years ago for making her relationship with her now-husband possible at all:

If I hadn't let myself go to those emotional depths, I wouldn't have been able to recognize the other people, creative outlets, and aspects of myself that were as compelling as the love I felt for my sweetheart. I didn't choose that approach, but it worked for the best—for me and eventually for my relationship. My strength ultimately allowed my sweetheart to show his vulnerability and those changes led to our ultimate union. Today, our marriage is solid, resilient, still intensely romantic—a study in the melding of personal freedom with marital devotion.

If you and your ex do decide to get back together, you may discover that, having arranged your life as a single person, it may be logistically difficult to reunite. Vaughan explains that separation is a lot of work. Telling everyone about the breakup and dealing with everyone else's reaction can be draining. Changing the patterns of our daily life to accommodate the changes a breakup can bring demands energy and constant negotiation. Once you've found a new home, reorganized your material world, and developed a separate social life, getting back together becomes more and more difficult.

Twenty-five-year-old Veronica's partner of three years broke up with her during his parents' bitter divorce. When they reunited a year later, she found that it wasn't as easy as she'd thought it would be:

Once we made the decision, we had to tell everyone. Some of my friends felt leery of our getting back together—they were worried that he would hurt me again. It took some time for them to accept that this was what I really wanted, what was best for me. And then we had to figure out where to live. I stayed with him and his roommates for a few months until we could find a place of our own. It was a hassle to have to move around all over the place, just to get back to where we'd been before we'd broken up. It took a long time before we got comfortable again in our life together.

While getting back together with an ex-lover is a viable option for some, Lucy told us about nearly getting back together with her most recent ex for the wrong reasons:

I was so scared about being on my own, and he just kept pursuing me. Suddenly, he was talking about his emotions, really trying to connect to me, sending me flowers, setting aside time for us to really talk. I was thinking about giving in for a little while, it would have been so easy. But ultimately I realized that people don't change overnight, and I wasn't in love anymore with the person he really was. The only reason I was even considering it was because it hurt so much—I wanted it to stop hurting so I could have my life back again. But finally I told him it just wasn't going to happen—and I'm so glad I did.

Talk of the Town

Once you've done the work of rebuilding your life and settling in, you may find that the people in your life have some reactions to all of the changes you've undergone. Barbara discovered that some of her friends were angry and anxious when she began dating a man, afraid that she wasn't going to be the "Barbara" they knew and loved:

When my friend Diane found out she was like, "Why do you have to be with this man? Come back to women, Barbara!" She was pissed off that I was with this guy.

The friend that introduced me to my new love was very upset, and I had a long talk with her. We took a long walk and she said that our friendship was irreparably damaged and might not even be viable anymore. She said, "My friendship with you was as a lesbian, and now your identity has changed and I don't know what that means to our friendship. So I just feel like I've lost a friend."

I was incredibly hurt and pissed at the same time. That whole year was not only spent starting a relationship with someone very different—a man—but mourning the relationship with Maggie and also mourning the change in my identity. Because people looked at me like I was a straight woman when I was with this guy. And it was really hard to be seen that way, and not to be seen fully for who I am. And at the same time, not being seen for who I am by these friends of mine who saw me as someone who had abandoned "the cause."

I think initially they thought I was experimenting. And I think that initially I thought I was experimenting. I thought, "Who knows what will happen. I can always go back to women." And I think he was aware of this, too. He didn't want it to just be a test.

I remember, I was so enmeshed in that lesbian world, that after the first time I went back, and he picked me up at the airport and tried to hold my hand, I totally freaked out. I had just come from a place where my identity was a lesbian, I felt really weird being seen with this man. I pulled my hand away 'cause I didn't want anybody to see me all of a sudden with a man.

It can be incredibly hurtful when the people you love don't support the changes you've undergone. The rippling effect that a breakup causes can continue to affect your community long after you've left ground zero and done the work of rebuilding. Lily didn't feel comfortable sharing everything about herself with some members of her community:

The day we broke up, I told my dad that one of the problems in my relationship had been that I'd realized I was bisexual. It was strange, because I could tell it was a shock to him, but the intensity of the breakup overshadowed everything else. We're really close, so it was a relief to me that he knew. He's been supportive, though it still seems sometimes like he loves me despite the fact that I'm a lesbian.

The rest of my family is pretty conservative. I really don't know if they'd continue to love and accept me if I told them. I've always been sort of a good girl—I've always wanted them to be proud of me. So it's terrifying to think that these people who've been such an important part of my life could just cut me off because of who I want to be with. For now, I'm sorta going by that "don't ask, don't tell" policy with them.

Hannah talked about how her community was responding to the life she was starting to build with her new partner:

I found that everyone was reacting to my new relationship based on the old one. I felt like my mom kept warning me to be careful, watch out in case he turns out to be like Scott. I had close friends who seemed ready to embrace anyone who seemed likely to commit to me, because I'd been so hurt when Scott hadn't. I know that they were all just trying to look out for me, but it was difficult to have my new relationship be judged in reaction to the one I'd left.

As for Scott, I think it really bugged him at first that I had someone new. We'd committed to staying friends, but this definitely challenged both of us. And it irritated me when Scott put it exclusively in terms of sex. He told me he was really upset when he realized I was sleeping with someone new, as if my new emotional involvement didn't matter. I think he just didn't want to deal with the reality that I was falling for someone else, so he had to restrict himself to thinking about it in terms of sex only.

Lynn found that the pain of her breakup had strengthened her bond with her parents:

They're really supportive. They think that what she put me through was ultimately the best thing that could have happened to me because of all the ways I've grown. My dad even consoles me, "Don't worry, you'll meet Mrs. Right"—I had to correct him, "Miss Right, I'd like her to be unmarried, thank you very much!" My mom even walked in the pride parade with me, largely due to the aftereffects of the breakup on the family.

Clare's family was a little shocked by her fierce postbreakup independence:

I've always sort of done things my own way, but after my breakup, I just went for everything I've always wanted. My family tried to convince me not to move across the country by myself, to stay close to them and go to graduate school there. But I knew I had to do it on my own. Now that I've done it, and I talk about how I want to do travel nursing and go all over the country and the world, they don't even bother trying to talk me out of it. They know I'm my own person, and that I'm going to pursue all of the adventures I've always wanted.

Keep On Keepin' On

The growth we've achieved and the knowledge we've gained about relationships and ourselves can help us hold on to the benefits of our breakups. With some conscious effort, we can continue to stay true to ourselves and, if we so choose, to build a new healthy and sustaining romantic bond that will allow us to continue to grow, rather than limiting our scope. Sarah had some advice on how to do this:

Be sure to reserve some significant space in your life for yourself. It's so tempting to continue to lose yourself in love, which I think is a pretty intoxicating thing. But it's even lovelier to actually be the kind of person that you like.

In addition to holding on to the benefits of our breakups, author Marny Hall explains why we must let go of the pain and fear that our breakups have caused:

> As long as we allow breakup terror to shape all our tomorrows, our own ability to storytell whatever future we want will be sadly limited. We will find ourselves dotting the *i*'s and crossing the *t*'s of our new love stories before we have even met out partners-to-be. Because of our anxiety, we dare not even ask ourselves the question that is at the heart of every good love story: what happens next? We are terrified that we *know* what might happen next. But this eagerness to avoid catastrophe doesn't keep us safe. It only robs our love stories of suspense, mystery, and romance. (74)

Chapter 8

Coming Home to Yourself

I don't feel like I'm half of something now. I feel like I'm just me. . . . I trust myself a lot more now—the decisions I make, the things I do day to day and the big things.

—Miranda

I realized from my breakup that I could love, really, really love—something I had doubted before; I could take care of myself; pain wouldn't kill me—I would get through it; and that love is worth the pain, in the long run.

—Joy

The breakup was like an earthquake, turning up the ground and exposing hidden places to the sun, allowing new growth. And with all the shifting and settling, the landscape of my life changed into a better place.

—Marilyn

As you find yourself settling in to your new life, your breakup may seem a million miles away, as though it happened a long time ago. You may have gone through so much change since those early days that ground zero is just a hazy memory. And your early efforts at rebuilding may seem like they happened to a different person. You may not even think about your breakup much anymore, busy in the life you've created. But it's a good idea to take some time to reflect on your past relationship and your experience of the breakup itself. Whether or not you've found some kind of closure that seems final, taking stock of where you've been, where you are, and how you got here can help you reap the full growth potential of your breakup, sending you into the future on the momentum of the positive movement you've achieved.

Was It for the Best?

Every one of the women we interviewed had positive things come from their breakup. The demolition that a breakup causes can provide the space and initiative to create dramatic change. Simone's breakup resulted in the loss both of her partner and the community of people in which they met, which she now believes was a cult. Though she was still in the rebuilding stage of her breakup when we talked to her, she could already see the good aspects:

For me the breakup was definitely positive, even though at the time it seemed like the worst thing in the world. But how could I have gone on with that relationship? Thank God I broke up with him because he was keeping me in the group. And it took all of that horrible breakup stuff for me to realize what the whole thing was—what he really was, what the group really was, how I'd betrayed myself, everything. So I'd have to say it was positive even though it was so painful.

Especially in long-term relationships, it's common to get stuck in ways of being or behaving that are ineffective or cause you distress. Maria's breakup forced her to change in ways she now appreciates:

It made me grow up emotionally. Before that I think my emotional world was a little narrow: "This is what I feel. Therefore you should give me this, and if you don't, I'll bang my head against the wall." And it was pretty miserable. A pretty miserable method of dealing with myself. I've come to a much, much better place than that emotionally. Now, what other people do has much less potential to throw me off balance. I feel more peaceful. And I think without that incredible pain I wouldn't have had the motivation to change. Without that I would still be hitting my head against the wall, sealed off from the world outside of me.

Most of the women agreed that when you're in the thick of grieving your breakup, it can be difficult to believe that the pain you're experiencing is a catalyst that will move you toward a more fulfilling life. But once you've been through most of the experience, it may be easier to identify the positive changes that have resulted from your breakup. Erin talked about how she's been able to shift her priorities to nurturing herself:

I'm starting to really love myself again—rediscovering the parts of myself I didn't like because they made me insecure and nurturing them because they're so important and definitive to my personality. I'm doing things for myself now—going to a gym, taking better physical and emotional care of myself and my friends. I spend more one-on-one time with the people I want to get to know better. I'm becoming a central part to a beautiful ring of friends. I'm finally finding my own, wonderful, grounded life here. And the only thing that can happen is growth.

Whether you've made changes in your emotional health, life philosophy, social life, or material world, allowing yourself to focus on these positive changes can be a freeing experience.

A breakup can also trigger the grieving of other losses you haven't yet processed. When Kris' partner left her for another woman, she was thrown into the chaos of ground zero but experienced positive outcomes from this emotional turmoil: "In a way I could say that I wished the breakup had happened a lot sooner, because it made me grieve my mother's death, which had happened a few years before, and I grieved a lot."

Just coping with a breakup itself can be an emotionally trying experience. But, as Maria found, once you've reached the settling in stage, you may recognize that what seemed unbearable was a necessary component in reaching the place you're at today:

In most relationship breakups you find out what you can do better with your life. You're bound to grow from it. You look at how you can do better, how you can listen to yourself more, and this is going to lead to a quantum leap in your development. The future is bound to be better, because you come to a real deep understanding of yourself as a result of this.

Miranda talks about how her breakup led her to see herself differently:

I don't feel like I'm half of something now. I feel like I'm just me. . . . I trust myself a lot more now—the decisions I make, the things I do day to day and the big things.

Lily feels that her breakup provided her with the ideal circumstances for positive growth:

There's something about this process that allows you to understand what you need and then begin to meet those needs, which I think is harder to do within the context of a relationship. I mean, in a relationship, when you realize you want something different, you have to negotiate, change the patterns you've set up with your partner. When you're single, you have space to re-envision everything—you have so much more room to maneuver.

Knowledge Gained Is Knowledge Earned

Breakups are a time when you get to know yourself better—who you are alone, what you want out of your life and your relationships. While this self-awareness is gained through a painful experience, it's the most positive benefit a breakup can offer. Eden, who eventually got back together with her ex, talks about the year they spent apart:

Without that time in Santa Cruz, I don't think I would be who I am, in terms of my sense of feminism, in terms of my ability to be honest with myself. I don't think that I would know who I was in the same way that I do if I hadn't spent time away from my big relationship.

The surge of independence and freedom that often comes with a breakup can change your self-concept. The process that you've been through may forever alter how you see yourself, your partners, and your community.

Surviving the ground zero chaos of a breakup and plunging into the rebuilding process can be a heady experience. Many women find that they come to a place where they understand and respect themselves more than before and make changes accordingly. Eden's breakup gave her the confidence to decide how she wanted to be treated by others. She said:

The biggest thing I learned was that I didn't have to take any shit from anybody ever. I just remember coming back and being so much more surefooted and so much more aware of my own strength.

Experiencing the intense emotions often resulting from a breakup can also affect how you feel about other people. You may find that your experience has allowed you to feel more compassion for the emotional pain others experience. When asked what she's gained from her breakup, Lynn said:

My ability to communicate and relate to people from a heart place. I don't know how on earth I would be going through training as a therapist from where I was before. That experience and where it took me was very important, in terms of helping me feel comfortable enough to really sit still, hearing how other people feel and really understanding their pain.

Whether in your personal or your professional life, your breakup may have left you with skills that you hadn't had before. You may find that you treat others differently because of what you've been through.

Perhaps the person you relate to better now is yourself. Kris said:

In the last two years I've gotten much more of a sense of who I am and what I want and what matters. The big change is that I've been allowing myself to have more things, giving myself more things than I did before. I'm feeling more compassionate with myself now.

Jeanette talked about the steps she took to better understand and take care of herself:

I talked to my friends about my relationship and my breakup over and over, bouncing ideas off of them. I went to therapy and really worked to rid myself of old baggage and allow myself to have the life I want. I wrote about my feelings and tried to think about them and work through them. And it helped me know myself better. I still have to consciously remind myself to take care of my emotional and physical well-being, but at least now I'm more forgiving of my flaws and I try not to criticize myself as much. And I'm still working on the changes in myself that my breakup instigated, even though it's no longer about the breakup.

When asked if she sees herself any differently now, Hannah said:

I feel stronger, I feel more confident. I know now that I have the support I need and the willpower to do what I want to do with my life. I never want to lose that conviction.

Joy talked about what she learned from her breakup:

I realized from my breakup that I could love, really, really love— something I had doubted before; I could take care of myself; pain wouldn't kill me—I would get through it; and that love is worth the pain, in the long run.

Clare acknowledged the active role she took in her breakup process, saying, "I've learned so much in the past year. And I know exactly how I've changed, because I've made it happen."

Hannah shared how she tracked her progress after her breakup:

Every few months or so, I'd just ask myself: "What do I know now that would've helped me then?" I did that recently and the answer was: I wish I'd known then how powerful I am. How powerful and strong I've discovered I am. If I'd known that then, I would've done so many things differently—but at least I know now!

When they were in the midst of ground zero, many of the women we talked to found themselves thinking, "How am I going to make it?" or "Things are never going to be the same." When they reached "the other side," the women who had rebuilt and settled into their lives were able to look back and recognize the strength and endurance that they'd always had. Acknowledging this power made many of the women feel that they would be able to face future difficulties with even greater courage.

Focusing on the gains that resulted from her breakup helped Renee let go of the past. She found that simply having endured the pain of her breakup helped her let go of her fears of abandonment:

I got that big question answered: Will I survive if something happens to my partner? I found out I am incredibly strong. I feel like what I survived was pretty horrific, and if something else comes along that's as horrific, I found out I'll be able to make it.

Like Renee, many of the women we spoke to learned things about themselves and their relationships that changed the way they would see romantic and platonic connections in the future. For Eden, it's her notions about what a breakup means that have changed. She said:

It's so personal when you break up. It's like flat-out devastation and rejection. But after a few years, you realize it's not necessarily that there's something wrong with you or your partner, but that there was just something wrong with the dynamic between the two of you.

While not everyone comes to a place where they can see their relationship in this light, many of us find that our breakups have taught us new ways of looking at relationships that allow us to let go of blame and move forward.

The knowledge gleaned from breakups isn't always about yourself or your romantic partnerships. Often your expectations and desires for your relationships with friends and family continue to shift long after a breakup. Eden said:

It wasn't until I was contemplating reuniting with my ex that I realized how much I'd changed. The most important thing that I'd learned was that my relationships with women count. I'd been really brainwashed about what I could expect from female friends, and those relationships—both with women and men—I made lasting relationships that I still feel are totally pivotal in my life. And actually, one of the friends I'd met while I was away for that year we were broken up married Craig and me—he was the officiator of our wedding. And that felt absolutely right, because I'd been friends with him at that time when I was learning about relationships that were all about respect and not about humiliation.

Erin talked about how the pain of her breakup has been one of her greatest learning experiences:

Every experience is a learning experience, and the most painful ones are often those that teach us the most. Who knows why that is, but it rang incredibly true in my experience. It was so awful and painful, and I wouldn't ever want to relive it, but I also wouldn't erase it from my past, because I have emerged more sure of myself and my values and self-identity, and I have emerged stronger. I wrote a line in a poem once, that I really feel is true of situations like this: "It is only through our tears that we see clearly."

New Perspective on Life

Once our world is moving in real time instead of "breakup time," we may feel as if we're seeing life in a whole new way. Denise said:

I've experienced grief in a way I've never felt before, and now when I drive down the street and I see the trees blooming I actually notice it, and I don't think I would've noticed that before. It's just different—my whole life—I'm living in color now, not just black and white with the occasional sunshine.

At the end of a long period of grieving, it can feel as if our life has been returned to us. Many of the women we spoke to said that in the settling in stage they felt excited about the new possibilities they were facing and relieved to finally be moving on.

Daphne talked about how her breakup has changed her outlook on life:

I feel much more spontaneous about life, about the choices I have. I'm thinking of myself, for the first time, as a single person who can do a lot, achieve a lot. Before I was always miserable because I wasn't in a relationship. And I feel like when I do get in a relationship again, it's going to be different. I'm not going to pin all of my hopes to it. I'm not going to give up everything and expect that the other person is going to provide everything.

Marilyn, who is now reunited and married to her ex-partner, explained how her breakup made way for dramatic changes in her life:

The breakup was like an earthquake, turning up the ground and exposing hidden places to the sun, allowing new growth. And with all the shifting and settling, the landscape of my life changed into a better place.

Using Your Own Natural Resources

One of the benefits of being single after a breakup is that we can put all of our time, energy, and other resources into taking care of ourselves. We can make choices that best suit us, without having to consider the needs of a lover. Jeanette, who was in a relationship that lasted through her high school and college years, said:

Everything is about what you want: What you eat for dinner. What you get when you go grocery shopping. What movies you rent. Where you want to live. How you want to spend your time. For the first time in my life, I had the freedom of being a single adult. I hadn't realized how much I'd been putting into that relationship. Being able to focus that energy solely on myself allowed me to make changes in my life that I never would've even considered before.

In the give-and-take of relationships, it's common to have to spend time doing things you don't particularly enjoy to please your partner, leaving you with less time to do the things you really love. Lee found not having to do this one of the best side effects of her breakup:

You don't have to compromise for a little while. My ex and I had a lot of things we really didn't agree on, like music and movies. Not having to worry about that has been such a gift. And just reading books you want to read, and hanging out with friends where before maybe not everybody got along—all of that is great.

Eden originally experienced this release of responsibility as symbolic of her single, and lonely, state. But she was eventually able to revel in the freedom of considering her needs as primary:

Always having to be considerate of someone else is such an incredible bummer. It's such a responsibility. So the potential for feeling free is limitless if you break up with someone. When you're with someone, you have to account for your behavior several times a day. "I'm going to the store, do you want anything?" or "I need to go to bed early," or "I'm going to take a shower." I mean, I told him when I took a shower, because what if he had to go to the bathroom or something?

Just being selfish for a little while, doing things for yourself without thinking about doing it for someone else, too, can be a relief. Lucy talked about one of the ways she enjoyed her newfound freedom: "Buying food just for yourself, like ice cream, instead of thinking, 'Oh, I'd better get him some, too.'" Sometimes it's the tiniest things that can make us feel free. Not having to consider a partner's needs, if only for a short time, can give us the chance to really focus on ourselves.

One of the most frequently mentioned benefits from a breakup was the time that it freed up. Indigo said:

I had time to put me at the center of my life. It was totally different. There was time to do what I wanted to do. There was time to take meditation classes, and I could roam around without answering to anyone or being home at a certain time. It was just great! That sense of being my own person was really freeing and marvelous to me.

Especially when you're in a long-term relationship, it's easy to forget what it's like not to have to account for your whereabouts to anyone else. Jeanette said:

Whenever I want to go out and meet new people or hang around with friends, I can. I used to totally plan my schedule around Chris. Now, I make my own decisions about how I'm going to spend my time.

After a breakup, you may see things about your relationship that you never noticed at the time, such as the extent of the compromises you made during your relationship. Eden, who eventually reunited with her ex, found that these revelations were crucial to her relationship today:

I was always sort of chasing after Craig, only having free time when he had scheduled something. It's humiliating to admit it, but I think that happens all the time, and I think it's one of the first things that you sort of discover when you break up. It's like, "Oh, my God. How much did I defer to their time and their needs?"

After we broke up, at first it was really lonely. But as soon as I realized the endless freedom I had, I actually enjoyed my time alone. I went bike riding all the time; I ate in restaurants he would have hated. I could do whatever I wanted without having to get "clearance."

Now that we're back together, we've consciously decided to always try and honor each other's autonomy. We're very specific about not giving each other shit when we can't spend time together. It's sort of become the hallmark of our relationship. It really had to change because I'd grown up so much when we were apart that there was no way I could—or would—defer to him the way I had before.

Clare talked about how she uses her time differently now that she's single:

I have a lot more time for myself. Reading, art projects, going out to the theater, music. All that great stuff, that, for some reason, I never did before.

Joy talked about using her newly freed time to nurture herself:

I'm better at spending time with myself, at taking care of myself. I eat better and sleep more. I do what I want to do and justify my actions to no one but myself. I've always known that I am a good friend and lover to others; now I'm a good friend and lover to myself. I'm enjoying this.

Another resource that becomes more available after a breakup is psychic space—the ability to think about other things besides your ex and your breakup. Simone said:

All that anxiety about whether or not he was going to call is gone. You know, at work I was always checking my home answering machine to see if he'd called. And, at the time, I would do a lot of things to get away from that feeling, but I was still always thinking of him. And now I don't have to.

Nikki talked about how this psychic space allowed her to rediscover her independent self:

I think women tend to blend their lives so much. We're naturally friends, we often think in a similar way, we do a lot of the same things, we share clothes. You can really lose your autonomy. So now I feel like I'm getting myself back. That's the fun part.

Free for All

One of the best parts of settling in to your rebuilt life is looking back and realizing the gains you've made. The women we spoke to seemed excited when talking about the benefits they'd gotten from the postbreakup process—everything from the freedom to be more themselves to the resolve to change their careers.

An important benefit most of us feel we gain as a result of our breakups is a sense of personal freedom—an increased awareness of what we want as women and the strength and resolution to get it.

Anne talked about the way she used her breakup to improve her relationships with herself and others:

I've been learning to set more boundaries—learning to say what I want. So, what I gained from the breakup is learning more about who I am and what I want. Having the opportunity to research that.

Our breakups allow many of us to become more clear about what we want from relationships and to make strides towards achieving those desires. Erin surrounded herself with people who supported the aspects of her identity that had been denigrated in her past relationship:

I spend more time with friends who give me positive feedback and who understand and support my bisexuality. I feel sexual and intelligent and attractive again. I love myself more, and therefore have more honest love to offer to others.

This is a time when many of us celebrate all of the aspects of ourselves that we appreciate and surround ourselves with others who support us in being our true selves.

One of the side effects of becoming "more yourself" is feeling more comfortable in your own skin. Sabine said that she finally enjoys going out alone now, where before she'd always wait for her partner or a friend to go someplace with:

I do a lot more on my own now that I finally feel settled again. If I'm in the mood to see a movie or go to a restaurant, I just go. It felt awkward at first, but now I really enjoy it. I'm not as afraid to spend time alone as I used to be, I think because I'm more comfortable with myself. I know myself better, so I don't need to be afraid that the second I let my guard down I'll see things about myself that I don't want to deal with.

Doing things alone doesn't only extend to seeing the occasional movie or going to a restaurant by yourself. Clare talked about her new willingness to travel alone:

I was thinking about going to Europe. Then I thought, "Do I really want to go by myself?" But, why not? All the other times I've traveled it has always been with one other person. I always thought that I needed one extra person there in case I need to make bail or something. But then you always have to compromise. I think I just might try it.

Many of the women we spoke to had grown to appreciate their time alone, giving them a greater sense of independence and confidence.

Even after we settle in to our lives again and enter a new relationship, we can still hold on to many of the freedoms we've earned. Indigo now has a relationship that involves a much greater level of independence than in her previous partnership. She said:

Because I have such an incredibly wonderful partner now, I don't feel that I have anyone holding me back or dragging me down—tugging at me in negative ways. I can do whatever I want. I can take classes without someone saying, "When are you gonna be home? Do you really have to go to the library?" I really feel now that I can do anything.

In addition to developing a stronger sense of independence after their breakup, many of the women talked about how their relationships with friends and family continued to thrive once their lives became more stable again. They learned that, not only can our friends and family help us through the hard times in our life, but they can also help us celebrate the wonderful times. Jeanette said:

At first, my relationship with my family and friends became closer because I needed their help to make it through a really awful time. But now that I've gotten to a place where I've experienced some closure on my past relationship and my breakup, I feel like my relationships are getting even stronger. I have more psychic space and energy to give to the people I love. It feels good to be able to connect with them from a stronger, more stable place in my life.

The rebuilding and maintaining of your community can enhance your feelings of self-esteem and autonomy, giving you a greater sense of personal freedom. Liza said:

I moved back to my hometown and made a whole bunch of new cool friends. Now I feel like I've been through enough breakups that I can get through anything and still be me at the end.

The sort of personal, emotional benefits women talked about seem to be some of the most powerful and important gains they made, affecting how they felt about themselves and their world.

Many of these personal gains translated into more specific, practical gains as well. Lots of the women we spoke to were able to achieve goals they'd never felt possible before. Elizabeth talked about the many things she's achieved since her breakup:

Regaining my individual identity was the foremost thing. But I also dove headfirst into a new career, starting a business with two friends. If I had still been with my ex, I wouldn't have pushed as hard to get the new business going, and I probably wouldn't have given it as much time or energy as it needed.

My whole life is different. In my current relationship, I am able to retain my identity and ask for what I need, and I have learned to compromise and even get some alone time, which I never had in my relationship with my ex.

I am more assertive, though still not as much as I should be, and more self-assured about my identity as a lesbian. My ex was my first lover and she spent a lot of time coaching me on how things should and shouldn't be. I'm much happier knowing many different kinds of dykes, who are living different kinds of lives. And of course, I have my business, I was able to finish school, and I have a "bigger" life in terms of the people I know and see.

The things you've learned about yourself can enable you to reach for goals and dreams with a greater intensity. Like Elizabeth, you may find that numerous aspects of yourself and your life have improved.

Marilyn's process of grieving opened her creative channels:

I started a journal of letters to him. I'd write my feelings, my anger, my frustration, passing along all my sisters' juicy insults, and would tell him I loved him more than I imagined loving was possible, and hated him for it. I wrote page after page, night after night, sitting out on my porch, and one night I decided the letters weren't for him, that this was a journal for myself. In retrospect, I think I had poured love into him that belonged to me, and once I stopped doing that I began to love myself more.

This became a blossoming time in my artistic life. I found a new reservoir of creativity. I began drawing and making fabric creations and discovered a more free-flow approach to writing. I think I became a better parent. Instead of waiting for this imagined wonderful father figure to fix our life, I accepted that I was to be a single mom, perhaps always, and that wasn't so bad. I developed close friendships with other moms, and some new routines—Tuesday nights out for Chinese dinner, daytrips on Sunday, and various events with another single-mom friend who liked to flaunt convention.

We'd cook hot dogs on the beach, kids bundled up, wind so high that the fire would go sideways and we'd have to move the hot dogs around to catch the flames.

Many of the women we spoke to took bold steps to change their jobs or career paths after their breakups. Daphne said:

I applied for this job in a field I'd never worked in and got hired. It's a whole new world, in a sense. The relationship just kept me very stuck, very paralyzed, because so much of my energy was going into trying to fix it all of the time.

The chore of tending to a failing relationship can be draining. Now that you're free of that, you can refocus your efforts in a variety of ways. Some of the women we spoke with recognized the possibility and jumped right on it. Lee talked about how she tried to maximize the time after her breakup:

I started my own business. I signed up for acting classes and auditioned for a play, all kinds of things I had kind of put on hold or was afraid to try. I just sort of said, "Hell, why not do it now?" The key for me was to do it right after the breakup, "Now is the time to do it, while I'm wanting to be strong, while I'm looking to get back to myself." You do it before you back out. You just sort of plunge into it.

One way to "plunge in" is to pursue work that you find fulfilling and meaningful, though simply having a job that financially supports you can be rewarding. Eden said, "I made my own money. It was the first time I'd really been on my own." Whether this is the first time ever or the first time in a while, being financially self-sufficient may be one of the practical benefits you earned through the postbreakup process.

When asked about what she'd achieved after her breakup, Maria said:

My job change, definitely. I didn't like what I was doing before and I was able to change it. My breakup has opened up so many more experiences and relationships to me. It's motivated me to actualize myself more in terms of changing my work. I was just content in the old relationship—I had little motivation to make changes outside. And suddenly my life's contentment started to depend on me, not on that relationship.

Jeanette, who is actively pursuing a career as a writer, talked about how her breakup allowed her to focus on her writing:

I never read or wrote for pleasure when we were hanging out, which was a lot of the time. I knew there was something wrong, that it was strange that I couldn't seem to do two of the things most important to me while I was with this person. After we broke up, I eventually started reading for pleasure, keeping a journal, that sort of thing. I recently had my first magazine article published. I never would have been able to do that the way I was in that relationship.

I feel like I've gotten back one of the most important parts of myself. It scares me that I gave that up before. I'm never going to let that happen again. I can see now that the only kind of relationship I want to be in is one where I can be the person I want to be and still be happy with another person—get support for my goals, not distraction from them.

Travel was also a common goal met in the postbreakup lives of the women we spoke to. Jeanette has traveled more since her breakup two years ago than she had in the rest of her life combined. She said:

The first trip I took, about four months after my breakup, was to visit my good friend whom I hadn't seen in about a year. I went to stay with her at her family's house in Hawaii. Just taking a week away, getting rest, being in a completely different, beautiful place, and getting her support was so helpful. It was the first time I'd felt alive in months. Since then, I've taken a road trip with one friend, went to Europe with another, and am planning a trip to D.C. and New York with another. I never would have done any of this before. It's all a result of my increased closeness with my friends and my new sense of adventure.

Even if it's just for a day, getting out of town can be just the trick when you need a change of pace. It doesn't have to cost a lot of money; the women we talked to did things like pack a picnic and go to a nearby park, beach, or reserve, or take a walk through parts of town they'd never really explored before.

You may be perfectly happy going to a neighboring scenic town, but you might also consider saving up (or using that nest egg) to go someplace or do something you've only dreamed of before. Renee said:

I've amazed myself with some of the vacations I've taken on my own. I've gone kayaking on the Sea of Cortez, I hiked in the wilderness of

British Columbia, and while I'm doing these things, I'm thinking, "My ex would be so amazed." But I'm also having a really good time. The social fabric of my life is completely different than it was. I spend time alone. There's a huge difference from who I was.

There's no time like the present to embark on your own adventures and achieve those fantasy goals that seemed impossible before.

Many of the women we spoke to have done a variety of things for themselves since their breakup. Hannah said:

Some of the wonderful things I've done since my breakup include writing a book; traveling to Europe with my good friend; making new, great friends; and adopting a new baby kitty all by myself.

Lynn worked through her grief by visiting some of the most beautiful parts of California and deciding to plant some roots, literally and figuratively:

In that first month and a half after the breakup, I hiked redwood forests and I went on a horseback trip in Yosemite. And I bought a house. I grew up moving around a lot, so I never thought I would settle in any particular place, and I'd always thought, "Well, I will if I meet somebody." Now I feel like it's perfectly okay to do it on my own. Soon I'm going to start planting the garden I've always wanted.

Veronica allowed herself to allocate time to do anything she wanted:

I don't know why, but going to a cafe by myself was so important to me. I got up on a Saturday morning at 7 A.M., hightailed it to my favorite cafe, and ordered breakfast, and I was just in my glory. It was a whole bunch of little things that I'd let go, like reading a book or singing in a choir. It was exciting that I had this free time.

The things you've achieved certainly don't have to be unusual or daring to be fulfilling. It's up to you to choose things that make you happy. Anne went back to an old habit she'd given up:

I'm reading now. My ex and I spent our time together, so reading kind of went out the door. But I love to read, so now I'm reading a book a week.

Clare has made a variety of practical gains that she feels good about since her breakup:

Going to nursing school, going to lots of new places (like taking the bus all the way to New Orleans), and launching a nursing clinic.

There are no limits to what you can do now. In response to other women's recounting of things that they've done, Jeanette exclaimed, "I love it! Breakups are good! Whoohoo!" Our sentiments exactly.

Welcome Home

As we finish settling in to our postbreakup lives, we have the opportunity to look back over how far we've come. Just as we once focused on the demolition and chaos our breakup brought to our life, we can now sit back and relax into a remodeled life of our own making. While your life may look vastly different from the one you'd once envisioned for yourself, you may have found—like the women we spoke to—that it's your new circumstances that now feel like home to you. And by holding on to the courage it has taken to make this life transition, you'll have the tools to do any renovating or repairs that come up in your future. You've done it once. Ain't no stopping you now.

References

Clunis, D. Merilee, and G. Dorsey Green. 1993. *Lesbian Couples: Creating Healthy Relationship for the '90s*. Seattle, Wash.: Seal Press.

Dockett, Lauren, and Kristin Beck. 1998. *Facing 30: Women Talk about Constructing a Real Life and Other Scary Rites of Passage*. Oakland, Calif.: New Harbinger Publications.

Edut, Ophira (ed.). 1998. *Adios, Barbie: Young Women Write About Body Image and Identity*. Seattle, Wash.: Seal Press.

Gilligan, Carol. 1993. *In a Different Voice: Psychological Theory and Women's Development*. Cambridge: Harvard University Press.

Hall, Marny. 1998. *The Lesbian Love Companion: How to Survive Everything from Heartthrob to Heartbreak*. San Francisco: HarperSan Francisco.

Hegelson, Vicki S. 1994. Long-Distance Relationships: Sex Differences in Adjustment and Breakup. *Personality and Social Psychology Bulletin* 20:254–265.

Jay, Karla, ed. 1995. *Dyke Life: From Growing Up to Growing Old, A Celebration of the Lesbian Experience*. New York: Basic Books/HarperCollins.

Koman, Aleta. 1997. *How to Mend a Broken Heart: Letting Go and Moving On*. Chicago: Contemporary Books.

Levinson, Daniel J. 1997. *The Seasons of a Woman's Life*. New York: Ballantine.

McDaniel, Judith. 1995. *The Lesbian Couples' Guide: Finding the Right Woman and Creating a Life Together*. New York: Harper Perennial.

Pam, Alvin, and Judith Pearson. 1998. *Splitting Up: Enmeshment and Estrangement in the Process of Divorce*. New York: Guilford Press.

Putney, Richard. 1981. Impact of Marital Loss on Support Systems. *The Personnel and Guidance Journal*. 351–354.

Radford, Barbara, Dianne Travers-Gustafson, Connie Miller, Claire L'Arcgevesque, Elizabeth Furlong, and John Norris. 1997. Divorcing and Building a New Life. *Archives of Psychiatric Nursing* 5:282–289.

Vaughan, Diane. 1990. *Uncoupling: Turning Points in Intimate Relationships*. New York: Vintage Books.

Viorst, Judith. 1986. *Necessary Losses: The Loves, Illusions, Dependencies, and Impossible Expectations That All of Us Have to Give Up in Order to Grow*. New York: Fireside.